Broken to Blooming:

A Flower Does Not Bloom In A Day

By

Ellie Palma-Cass

Broken to Blooming:

A Flower Does Not Bloom In A Day

By

Ellie Palma-Cass

EDITED BY DBC AGENCY WRITERS
USA

Broken to Blooming

First Published in 2015 by Ellie Palma-Cass.

Scripture taken from the Holy Bible, NEW INTERNATIONAL VERSION®, NIV® Copyright © 1973, 1978, 1984, 2011 by Biblica, Inc.®.Used by permission. All rights reserved worldwide.

ISBN 978-1-312-82890-2

Official Website: www.elliepalmacass.com

ORDERING INFORMATION: Special discounts are available on quantity purchases by corporations, associations, educators, and others. For details, please contact:

Agent: DBC Agency Writers
901 N Brutscher Street
D-180
Newberg, OR
97132, USA
E-mail: dbcagency@outlook.com

Front & Back Cover Design: LLC Designs©2015

Dedication

To my very precious daughter Rhiannon. You are my heartbeat; my everything here on earth and, words can't ever describe the depth of my love for you; the awe and wonder at your insight into the real issues that matter and your inquisitive and growing faith in our Lord Jesus Christ.

Oh, how you make me smile with pride, giggle with our inside jokes and laugh hysterically at times when I need to laugh the most!

You are the meaning of the word 'blessing' and *I love you* angel face!

We'll always be the Palma-Cass girls!

I pray all the desires of your heart are fulfilled and that you will always be 'blooming' wherever you are on your journey.

Love you more, love you most

Mum x

Contents

Acknowledgements

To all the staff at DBC Agency Writers for the hours of work put into promotion and development of this work. You are dedicated beyond words.

To LCC Designs for designing the book cover and sticking to every detail I wanted! Thank you!

With Special Thanks

To AK Chenoweth, for your dedication, selfless commitment and ingenious business acumen. You are an amazing woman who advised me and navigated this whole process for me. As I have written this book, you have been my midwife; with me through growth, labour and finally birth. I am so thankful for the advice and support in writing, re-writing, editing, and re-editing! Phew! You are a God ordained friend and sister in Christ. Thank you!

To 3-in-1 Global Prayer Network, USA. You have enveloped me in prayer and provided spiritual nourishment. We know the enemy did not want this book to come to fruition but we know the Lord reigns! I am ever grateful for the gentle, prayerful balm of 3in1 GPN. God bless all of you!

To Andrina Sharples, the glamorous blonde who was obedient to Christ. Because of that obedience, I was saved for eternity. I love you. Thank you!

To Terry Rossington, the most loving, gentle and caring man I know. You took on the very difficult role of 'father' to me here on earth, by order of our Father in Heaven. Thank goodness, you have been able to watch me go from 'broken' to 'blooming'. I have no doubt it is through the love you and Linda (RIP) have poured into me. I love you.

And, last, but never least, to all the adored, cherished, and beautiful friends in my life. You know who you are and I can't mention names because there are too many! That's how good our Lord is! He 'sets the solitary in families'. I love you so much and I thank God every day for you. God bless you all!

Endorsements

This is clearly a compelling story of God's grace and love pouring into Ellie's life and changing her forever; written in an articulate and heartfelt way. I have no doubt it will particularly minister to many broken women and inspire their journey to wholeness.

PASTOR PHIL PYE
NATIONAL LEADERSHIP TEAM, ASSEMBLIES OF GOD
UK

As I read the first few pages, I felt moved to tears. Then a few pages later I was at peace, then basking in God's love and then thrown right back to the experiences of my own, at times nerve-rackingly similar, childhood - I was hooked! Ellie hides nothing. We are honoured to share her most personal testimony and through this, it has enabled us to understand why she is the woman she is today. Her testimony resounds from the place of, '……When I am weak, then I am strong…..' Thank you so much Ellie for sharing, this book will bring much needed healing and clarity to many!

ELDER SONIA C HOGG
RUACH CITY CHURCH, LONDON
UK

Ellie is one of a kind. She is the kind of person who is easy to love. The story of her life so far is compelling, honest and littered with grains of wisdom. Whether you hear her story through this book or first hand in a live setting, you will be struck by how impactful her experiences are and how grateful she is to still have the opportunity to celebrate life itself. Women like me, enjoy her raw energy and sense of fun. In fact, I can't think of many times she hasn't put a smile on my face. She makes things happen and she makes things take second place to people. I hope this book encourages many to go after their dream, no matter what gets in the way. Read Ellie's life story and be inspired.

SANDRA GODLEY
INTERNATIONAL AWARD WINNING VOCAL ARTIST
www.sandragodley.org

We found *Broken to Blooming* poignant, introspective, challenging and pulled from the depth of Ellie's being. It is extremely well written and fast paced so that the reader wants to know more; wants to help Ellie escape the intolerable situation. The Scripture gives great hope and is a necessary relief to the pathos. This book speaks to far wider an audience than we all wish were true. But the reality is such abuse is far too common and far too suffered in the loneliness of an impotent child. Therefore, it is not only a 'well-written 'exercise in personal healing; it will be a tool for many people to know and experience that inner healing through Ellie's writing and sharing. We hope she will share more with us

ARCHBISHOP METROPOLITAN DOYLE VOLENTINE AND REVEREND CAROLYN VOLENTINE
ANCCI,
USA

I hope every reader of this book gets to meet Ellie. You will immediately, be overwhelmed, by her depth of warmth and love. She wears a glow that sparkles like a diamond; however, every diamond has its own story and process to go through before it begins to shine. This great book will take you through Ellie's unique journey and when you have finished reading, you will understand why she is able to sparkle like a diamond.........Ellie, you are an inspiration; thank you for sharing your heart.

PASTOR SANDRA DAWKINS
ALL NATIONS FOR CHRIST, DERBY, UK
www.anfc.org.uk

The title *Broken to Blooming* is indeed an understatement. Ellie's story is initially one of survival, surviving the despicable acts of an abusive and violent father - and becomes the joyous testimony of her miraculous transformation into the effervescent Ellie we all know and love now. A testimony to the keeping and saving power of a Heavenly Father. You'll understand where her passion for Jesus and people comes from after reading her story.

BILL PARTINGTON
UNITED CHRISTIAN BROADCASTERS, UK
www.ucb.co.uk

I was absolutely riveted by the first chapter of *Broken to Blooming* and brought to tears……….. However, I stand in awe at our great God and what He has done in, through and with Ellie's life. God truly gives us beauty for ashes! This book will impact people to the deepest part of their being when they realise that God, our God, can turn any bad situation around for good.

PASTOR ANN STRICKLAND
KINGS LIFE CHURCH,
UK

When Ellie asked me to have a peek review at her first book, *Broken to Blooming,* I felt honoured. As I read her testimony, I quickly realised how deeply open and vulnerably she tells us of the depth of her story as she jumps in, right from the onset - giving a brilliant picture of who she is, or was, and how she got from there to here today, through her passionate love for Jesus. This is an astonishing testimony of a survivor - an overcomer - a woman's life well worth reading about. Her writing style is easy to absorb and I look forward to hearing of much healing because of her willingness to tell her story of the power of love and forgiveness.

PASTOR JULIE ANDERSON
THE PRAYER FOUNDATION | THE DEBORAH COMPANY | COMMONWEALTH CHURCH,
LONDON, UK

Ellie's book is not only a powerful testimony of how God has set her free but also a reminder that children (and adults) go through the most horrific experiences and at times without it being noticed. This book will not only challenge you to your core but it will encourage you to bring your own hurts and pains to Father God who is, and always has been, Ellie's loving father.

PETER GLADWIN
AUTHOR OF OUT OF ASHES | FOUNDER OF OUT OF ASHES MINISTRIES
www.outofashes.co.uk

For Samuel Eliot William

My first born

My treasure

My stolen one

Until we meet again

I love you...

For my Lord

To my Lord and Saviour Jesus Christ
To God, my Father in Heaven
To Holy Spirit, my comforter
My husband, my brother, my friend, my all
Only you and I know how I really went from Broken
to Blooming. Thank you for your Living Water, for
quenching my desperate thirst, for shedding tears
with me, for never letting me go, for watering that
fragmented shoot.

I BLOOM FOR YOU!

Preface

Over the last few months, as I have written the words in this book; this testimony; I have had to relive portions of my life that were buried deep within my mind. Akin to a casket of pain hidden far below the earth, full of dust and rubble. To open that casket has been utterly painful and at times, I didn't believe I could dig inside it any further.

However, God used the whole process of writing this first book to finalise areas of healing. These areas had been buried so very deeply that I couldn't even have begun the healing process without yielding every word, every emotion, and every thought to God. Ultimately, it is that very process that I want to share with you.

There is no other way to heal from the past, than to receive the healing balm of Jesus. Many people in this world suffer the worst of degrading atrocities, and trauma can be experienced in differing levels, but to that one person, that one individual - pain is pain is pain. Whatever your story is, or has been, please know that the only way to complete healing is through our Redeemer, Jesus the Christ.

He is the source of every good thing and He is the only Way. Rooted in Him is truly the ONLY way to live a life of abundance and peace. I know; I continue day-to-day in the healing process. Because He is, I can.

Ellie

'They triumphed over him by the blood of the Lamb and by the word of their testimony; they did not love their lives so much as to shrink from death.' Revelation 12:11

Prologue

'She is clothed with strength and dignity; she can laugh at the days to come.' Proverbs 31:25

****

She sat in her little green car; an overflow of tears pouring down her cheeks, her chest, her body shuddering. Not constantly like before but with the occasional shake only a lament can bring. It wasn't a howl nor a wail anymore either; her body had finally succumbed to the deep rooted pain that had submerged itself far beneath the exterior wall of this woman; a wall that others would call flesh and bone. The pain and fear was so deep, so intense, that she could barely speak the words she wanted to say. She was spent, completely debilitated. The pain was physical and real. It caused her to not breathe at times. A lifetime of hurts and atrocities had hit her instantaneously and something had to give. Something inside of her knew and she sensed that these words had to be shouted out! These words had to be declared! They had to be roared! She would shout out these words as soon as she could, but right now, at this moment, she couldn't. Not even a whisper. She could not even form her lips to speak. There was torrential rain all around and she had driven into a huge park grounds with a vast and extensive depth of forest; towering trees that felt like a refuge; an immunity almost from herself; from whatever was causing this abysmal pain. Whenever she was amongst trees and nature she felt a calm. Nature reminded her of her grandfather. And rain; she loved rain. Still does. A joy arises in her to this day whenever there is a thunderstorm and the most tempestuous of weather.

But not that day.

That day turned out to be the catalyst. It was THE day; the turning point. The day in which all 29 years of grief, heartbreak, despair and fear had accumulated and had to be expelled. She was scared, very scared; almost panic-stricken. She was a physical and emotional mess and a concentrated mass of anguish, misery and wretchedness.

And so…………..she screamed out! To a God she didn't know. To a God she wasn't sure even existed! To a God who was waiting for His little girl………for THIS moment to arrive.

"HELP! I CAN'T LIVE ANYMORE. I CAN'T DO THIS 'LIVING THING'. I NEED IT ALL TO END AND I DON'T THINK I CAN STOP MYSELF BUT I CAN'T LEAVE MY BABIES. SO WHAT DO I DO? OH, PLEASE, PLEASE, WHOEVER, WHEREVER, ARE YOU THERE? HELP ME, HELP ME, IF YOU ARE REAL, IF YOU ARE LOOKING NOW, HELP ME! HELP ME PLEASE! DO SOMETHING PLEASE! PLEASE JUST HELP ME!"

And He did…………

"AND THE DAY CAME WHEN THE RISK TO REMAIN TIGHT IN A BUD WAS MORE PAINFUL THAN THE RISK IT TOOK TO BLOSSOM"

Anais Nin

Chapter 1: Rescue Me

'...who saves me from my enemies. You exalted me above my foes; from a violent man you rescued me.' Psalm 18:48

'Mum! Your tea is getting cold!'

You know what? That is the sweetest sound on this earth to me and it fills my ears at least once a day! My beloved daughter Rhiannon calls out to me from the kitchen and I smile at the thought of how she has grown in the last year. Immediately I get up from my office chair and join her for a much needed cup of tea. As I enter the kitchen, the half opened fridge door lights up her beautiful, radiant, innocent face.

'*It's over there*' she says pointing to my favourite, extra-large tea cup and saucer.

She rushes off in the direction of her bedroom to listen to some music and informs me that she is going to take a shower and then go to bed. I follow her and give her a kiss and a huge hug and thank her for my Earl Grey brew. She makes the best cup of tea in the world!

'*I'll pop in soon and we can pray before you go to sleep. Thanks again for the tea, sweetheart,*' I call after her as she disappears into her room. I never want Rhiannon to feel that she isn't loved immensely or unappreciated. It's hugely important to me.

I like to think that I'm a good mum, loving and caring and I hope that I am always doing the right thing by my daughter. I absolutely adore being a mother. It was, I firmly believe, implanted in me from before the foundations of the world were even set in place! I'm convinced of it!

As I contemplate how blessed I am to have Rhiannon in my life, I lift my hot, steaming cup and return to my cosy office. The sun is still managing to emit a warm glow even though it is almost the end of a beautiful summer's day. I stand for a moment soaking in the last rays that have chosen to bathe my room with their welcome arms.

'*What an amazing sight*,' I say out loud to myself, as I look across the town's skyline. I smile and close the door behind me. I am exhausted from a busy week in London; a culmination of numerous busy weeks. I log out of the computer and sit looking out of the window and with just the natural light for company; I switch off my study lamp.

A long shadow casts itself across the room and the sun has completely disappeared out of sight, but I am content and I am at peace. In the stillness of the moment I start to think back in time, to a place when everyone it seemed, except God, was in control of my life, and a darkened room offered nothing but fear and uncertainty.

****

My birth mother had experienced a privileged upbringing. She was privately schooled and her parents, my Grandparents, absolutely adored her. My most memorable thoughts of her are that she was extremely beautiful. She possessed the most amazing huge, green, piercing, almond-shaped eyes, high cheekbones and luxurious, dark, glistening hair. I remember as a young child rubbing my face in her hair. It was so soft and I recall vividly the distinct aroma of her expensive perfume filling the air around her; totally encasing me. It was here I felt safe and here I felt loved. My father on the other hand was an ex-army officer and unfortunately possessed very violent tendencies towards women. I would soon learn that being a girl would bring incomprehensible challenges.

I was only out of hospital, eleven days old in fact and my presence had barely been recorded here on the earth. My mother, like any young mother, was excited to bring me home and show me off to everyone, especially the grandparents but my father on the other hand, did not respond well to my presence. Indeed, he had a very different type of welcome awaiting me. What happened next is usually found in a report that embodies the news headlines and captures the general public's attention with horror. I had just been released home from the maternity home with my mother. In those days, the 1970's, mum and baby would spend approximately a week in hospital after the birth of a first child. I was extremely healthy and it was time for me to enter society!

There was a welcoming party at home. My maternal Grandparents ready to greet this new addition and my father hovering in the background. Call it jealousy or whatever psychological condition one wishes to diagnose, but to state that my father did not respond well to my presence would be a gross understatement. Indeed, he had a very different type of reaction. No sooner had I been released home after my birth than I was admitted to another hospital just a few days later. The reason? My natural father had slipped surgical spirit down my throat. I know that it is only by God's hand I survived as the amount could have left me with severely disabled organs. At the hospital he explained away the event as an accident and I was released again into my mother and father's care. Surgical spirit is a form of rubbing alcohol. It can cause blindness and it wasn't until many, many years later that I would have to return to the causes of a disease I had in one of my eyes. A disease that I was much too young to acquire even in adult years yet could be caused through head trauma in a young person or the intake of rubbing alcohol. It seems I would experience both.

And so this was how my life began.

****

'So we fix our eyes not on what is seen, but on what is unseen, since what is seen is temporary, but what is unseen is eternal.' 2 Corinthians 4:18

If my father's actions had been, as he had claimed, an 'accident' and, the subsequent events that followed were all misfortunes, then there would be no need for the early chapters of this book. My father had an appetite for destruction; an insatiable one. Carrying out violent acts against my mother was appalling itself but using a young baby and later, a young toddler, to continue this 'game' was another. His behaviour continually and persistently played out in a reality and in a variety of ways. It was made up with the ingredients of pain and horror; exposing my emotions and my mind to terrible traumatic incidents that would last long enough, to not only break my mother's spirit but almost literally destroy me. Fractured bones take only a few weeks to heal and it is a temporary state. However, when a spirit is disabled and fractured, I really believe that it cannot truly heal without the intervention of Jesus. The Bible teaches us that the things we can see are temporal but that which is unseen are eternal.

As the days, months and years passed, I became more like an object and a focus of rage for my father. He would use me as a facilitator for his rage and used me in acts of violence to dominate and manipulate my mother. She was in a fragile state of course and being young and afraid, would cower and tremble at this forced jurisdiction. I believe that my mother was hopeful she could avoid his fist. However, the sad truth is, that she rarely did and, regardless of how humble or should I say fearful she became before him, or how much she begged him to stop, he would not, and his heavy hand would come down hard upon her frame.

As far as I am concerned and with my knowledge of events, my tiny, vulnerable state did not have any sway with him. He was a tall, large man who would always come short of bearing his full strength against me, like a torture of sorts. He would constantly commit fearful acts of violence and aggression against my person. I may have been a very young child, but I possessed the capacity to feel, hear and remember.

My father liked to play games on a daily basis. His favourite was tormenting my mother by using violence against me. Firstly, he would secure the door of the nursery, locking my mother out, leaving me and him together. Then he proceeded to throw me up and down in the crib; one of his many twisted methods to try and silence my crying. My mother was completely helpless to stop him. She was on the other side of the door, hearing my cries and, in between my cries and my father shouting, she would hear the noise of my little body hitting the cradle.

Upon reflection, she must have been in a frenzied state of despair. Imagine hearing your husband shouting at the top of his voice, throwing your baby up and down in the crib and hearing the wails of your child and all along knowing that your efforts to intervene and break through the door to your baby would be futile. She was not able to stop him harming me and her pleas and cries for him to stop, would always fall to the ground, just like all the other times.

When I conceive of those times, although I was very young, I still feel I can hear the thudding on the door in my bedroom and I can still hear the desperate tones in my mother's voice. Yes; the urgency and panic of the situation saturates my soul to this very day. Hence, I cannot bear to think of any child suffering physical violence without thinking about it and experiencing the residue in my soul. This is one of the reasons my heart is intense with dedication and devotion to loving any child; in fact, any child of God, and that can mean a grown adult.

I truly believe she must have known as a mother, in her heart, that it would be only a matter of time. One shake too many or one more 'accident' and that would be it! Her precious baby would be gone.   Therefore, as you can clearly see my perception of what should have been a true, loving, stable family home ought to be, was tainted and twisted from the beginning.

How I didn't end up with any sort of attenuated damage at that time is really nothing short of a miracle but as I mentioned previously, some harm was done which wasn't revealed until many years later.

After I was saved, the truth was exposed finally and then it was clear that the enemy, who roams about like a roaring lion wondering who to devour, was on an all-out mission to kill me; because he knew God's plans for me and he was going to use every device to stop me achieving those goals! With the enemy working through my natural father he was ensuring that the path that God had intended for me to take would become more and more violent, warped and dysfunctional until I would, in the enemy's eyes, break.

People will argue that a small child or toddler cannot recall anything or very little detail at least. Here is where I have to totally disagree and I will describe an incident which occurred to me when I was only 18 months old to prove this very point. I can remember the Blue Willow design patterned side plate as though it was just yesterday. I can even remember the exact size of the plate. It was breakfast time and the flavours and aroma of eggs and the toast popping up from the toaster is still very vivid. My father was undoubtedly huge in comparison to me. His hands would easily eclipse mine and he was strong, very strong. On this one particular day I recall the sunshine lit up the kitchen and it warmed my face as I was placed on my 'high chair' and the illumination of the sun made me squint. My mother had made me some eggs for breakfast but on that day, like a typical choosey toddler, I didn't really want to eat them! At first my mother tried to persuade me but to no avail.

I was preoccupied with the heat on my face from the sun and the beautiful warm glow that made the usually darkened kitchen light up. My mother tried another couple of times and only smiled at my resistance.

My father soon noticed this and decided that *he* wanted me to eat the eggs and so he sat down beside me and lifted my fork. Placing a large piece of scrambled egg on it he started to force the fork into my mouth, hurting my lips and jarring the instrument right up into the roof of my mouth. It was so painful, I could hardly swallow and I struggled, crying between the mouthfuls. I could feel the weight of his hand each time prizing my lips open with the pronged end of the fork. I tried to not open my mouth but I could feel his big heavy warm hand against my wet cheeks and the cold stainless steel against the tender roof of my mouth. At that moment, suddenly, I accepted the pain, and I went into agreement with that which was being inflicted upon me. Somehow I knew deep within that I could make it worse if I resisted, so I stopped fighting and stopped resisting. This decision would have a long-term effect on my life.

To this day if I see that Blue Willow design, it takes me straight back to that time, when the warm glow of the sun on a summer's day was eclipsed by a large heavy hand. When a tiny toddler called Ellie, was totally defenseless with no sword nor shield.

In summary, in the first three years of my life the only days of peace I had experienced, were the first 7 days, when I was in the maternity home with my mother. The promise of a loving family and home was as far away as the sun that used to warm my face. It was an unreachable concept. There had to be a change or we wouldn't survive. The question poised, was it too late?

'In him we were also chosen, having been predestined according to the plan of him who works out everything in conformity with the purpose of his will,' Ephesians 1:11

Chapter 2: Questions, Questions but No Answers

'Though my father and mother forsake me the LORD will receive me.' Psalm 27:10

Days rolled into weeks, weeks into months and months into years and as I think back on that time, I thank God for protecting me and enabling me to survive. I could not have run away from home. I was only three years old and totally dependent on these two people for everything. Then one day, suddenly and without warning and, just when you thought this hopeless situation would end up as a tragedy, my mother, after three years of torment and abuse did the bravest thing in the world. She picked me up in her arms, walked out of the front door and for the very first time in my short life, the man of violence was behind me.

'You armed me with strength for battle; you humbled my adversaries before me.' 2 Samuel 22:40.

Now, I understand this, that there is a body of belief out there, comprising of Christians, who believe that you should stay with your spouse, <u>no matter what</u>! However, I can state with authority that no woman, nor indeed man, should have to put up with any sort of chronic violent and destructive behaviour from their spouse. This is particularly true whenever there are children involved. In 1 Peter there is a very important scripture,

'Husbands, in the same way be considerate as you live with your wives, and treat them with respect as the weaker partner and as heirs with you of the gracious gift of life, so that nothing will hinder your prayers.' 1 Peter 3:7

If you are in a marriage or relationship where you find you are constantly searching or waiting for this scripture to be made manifest, then you must examine yourself as well as the other person. Neither should you have to remind your spouse of this scripture either; it should already be a part of your lives, already a part of your marriage or relationship and bound by the Holy Spirit's covenantal relationship with you both. If you cannot love and respect your partner and can only offer criticism and abuse then you need to establish some form of Christian counselling. The foundational rules of co-existence are laid out by God; love, respect and honour. I truly believe that if God's rules are followed then peace will reign in your home.

Although my childhood was immersed in violence from the beginning, I was shown unconditional love through my maternal Grandfather. I thank God for him every day. When my mother had left my natural father, we were welcomed at my Grandparent's home. Although it would prove to be a temporary move, it was most welcomed and for the first time in my life, I felt free! My Grandad, as I called him, and I, had a unique and powerful Granddaughter/ Grandfather relationship. We spent a lot of time together and he made me feel loved and safe. I adored him. And that is the thing about love isn't it? It is eternal. It is more than an emotion and it is spiritual because <u>God is love</u>.

'Whoever does not love does not know God, because God is love.' 1 John 4:8

Grandad knew the name of every tree. There wasn't one that he did not know and I often reminisce of our times together. Those times, well they were precious. God ordained them and in the years ahead I would often 'use' them to help me through the most difficult of times. I know deep within my spirit that our relationship was just as important to Grandad.

As well as possessing a great knowledge of trees and nature, Grandad also had an extensive knowledge of birds and whenever they sang he could instantly identify them by their call. He would instantly identify them and tell me the type of bird that was calling. He possessed an eager interest of the world around us, of God's creation and it was like a breath of fresh air to me. It was so different from the darkened walls of my first home and the world that I had come to know as family. That world I dwelt within was like a black and white photograph, lifeless and bland. It was like God had flicked a switch and the world had become multicoloured and vibrant. I felt alive and fearless. I can recall, as an innocent child, watching him intently as he spoke about the birds and as a child I thought that he was actually communicating with them and vice versa! Perhaps they did! I yearned to become like my Grandad and become a female version of 'Dr. Doolittle,' but I never did, although in time, this notion became a great diversion for me.

I was eight years old and five years had passed, when my mother decided to buy her own house. It was an investment and a statement of independence on her part. She had also met a man from London and it wasn't long until he had moved into our new home. I was told that he wasn't allowed to see his own two little girls. At eight years old I didn't really have an awareness or understanding of what that meant or why and to be honest, I didn't really care either. The important thing was, he was available as a Dad for me and my mummy seemed happy. I liked the thought of being 'his daughter' and being special. For the first time I would have a real 'father figure' in my life. Grandad already had his place so hopefully, this man would be just like Grandad; kind and gentle as a Dad ought to be.   Initially I was very happy with our situation, although I do recall that whenever I was around him there were times when I had a strange feeling inside. I felt uncomfortable. It was not based on anything that had occurred but it was instinctive and quickly I would learn how accurate my instincts were...

****

This particular day my mum had got up at the usual time to make the breakfast. I stretched and yawned and began to open my eyes. The curtains were still closed in my bedroom and the light outside was stretching to try and get into the room! I got up and went to the bathroom and returned to my room. I was about to put on my dressing gown when the boyfriend came into my room unannounced. Suddenly and without warning, he started to take down his pyjama bottoms exposing himself to me. I felt strange. I didn't know whether to giggle or cry. However, when he saw my reaction, he slipped out of the room swiftly. I was in a state of shock and felt numb. I tentatively made my way to the door and peeked round the corner. He was gone and so I made my way downstairs to breakfast. I felt awkward and embarrassed but didn't really know why. I just had an instinctive awareness that what had happened did not feel right. As I sat down my mother offered me breakfast and for the first time since the incident I looked across the table at him. He returned my look and made eye contact with me. He looked at me with a strange gaze and it made me feel scared and intimidated. It was a different kind of 'scared' than I had experienced with my natural father. This was something else. This was a different type of fear; one that paralysed me.

That day was the beginning of what I can only describe as a series of molestations, violence and offences against my person, both physical and emotional, that would warp my entire relationship status with the opposite sex for many years to come. I did not possess the sexual awareness or understanding of an adult and I felt constantly threatened and trapped in my own home. I tried making things up to avoid being alone with him. I tried to feign illness but I was only a child and powerless.

My mother was oblivious of his behaviour towards me. She thought he was the 'salt of the earth' and eventually she married him. The day that they married and he officially became my stepfather, he took me to the side and said something very strange to me,

'Ellie, today I didn't just marry your mum. I married you too. Me and you are married'

A shudder ran up my spine and I felt as though I was chained to a wall with duct tape on my mouth. Unable to speak, I remember thinking, 'Yuck! I don't want to be married to you!'

Panic filled my soul at the realisation that this man was in our family for good and what he had been doing to me would intensify and get worse.

As time went by the perceived, idyllic marriage that my mother had hoped for disintegrated. My stepfather was an alcoholic and became verbally and physically abusive towards my mother. Between what I had witnessed her go through with my natural father and now my stepfather, it had tainted a lot of areas of my life, particularly the area of relationships with boys and men. These abhorrent acts of violence committed against my mother and myself made me feel unsafe, threatened and scared. I could sense my mother's primordial fear and it stuck with me.

Eventually my stepfather's addiction to alcohol got the better of him. He began spending every night in the local pub drinking away any money he had and it soon ran out. It got to the stage that he forced my mother to go with him to the local pub and bring her cheque book with her so as she could take over paying for his drink. I would be left alone in the house most nights whilst they went out for hours at a time. I regularly woke up at home alone and frightened because when I went to bed, mummy was there and when I awoke during the night it was pitch black and she would be gone. I was alone, surrounded by inky, lightless rooms in a dark, cold house with moving shadows.

One night in particular I awoke, stricken with panic and fear as I realised again, I was alone. I decided to go to look for my mummy. Where could she be? Why would she leave me alone? Was she ok? Had something happened? Questions, questions, but no answers. No one answered my questions that night or any night. I took a deep breath and put on my little nylon pink diamond-shaped patterned dressing gown. Barefoot, I gingerly descended the stairs. I was going to look for my mummy and I was going to find her!

I glanced over and across the room as the shadows on the walls from the street lights seemed to get larger and larger. I finally reached the phone and started to dial my grandad's number. A lady answered. I had obviously dialled the wrong number! However, this lady listened to me intently as I started to pour out my heart and my fears and the fact that I didn't know what had happened to my mother. She was so caring and spoke to me softly, ever so softly. She understood immediately what had happened. To this day her voice and tone is with me, comforting me and I often wonder who she was. She instructed me to call her back once I had been able to contact my Grandad, but of course I didn't know her number and there was no number saved in those days on the phone, so I was unable to fulfil her request and call her back.

Maybe she was a Christian and she prayed for me. I like to think she did because somehow from then on I knew I would be alright. I decided that the only alternative was to go to my mummy at the pub. So I began to walk up the long, darkened street and up a hill to the local public house where they were drinking. I took a deep breath and entered 'their world.' I walked through the heavy doors and into the smoky atmosphere. My eyes were stinging. I can still hear the loud raucous laughter as I recall this and the stench of spilt beer. Someone must have shouted out to my mother and stepfather because the next thing I knew, I was being pushed along the road. Both of them were yelling at me! When we got home my stepfather got out his leather belt and started to strike me with it across my bottom. I was being punished for getting them into trouble, as people were well aware I had been left home alone at such a young age. However, I just felt relieved that I wasn't in the house alone anymore. I preferred my mummy and stepfather being angry with me and therefore, I blocked out the searing pain I felt on my bottom. At least I was not alone anymore.

So what I can say of the incident with the phone? One thing I am certain of is this. That God sent me an angel in the darkness and just at the right time. I now know, on reflection many years later, I rang the correct number, at the right moment that night. As I look back, I am forever grateful to God for the answered prayer of an innocent, little frightened girl who was abandoned and lost in a darkened house. She may not have known who was in control of her life at that time, or indeed that her steps were purposed. Like Joseph in the Bible, she had been struck and punished by someone cruel and familiar, whose soul only emitted darkness. However, the kind, thoughtful and caring words of a stranger, will stick with her far longer than any belt. God is good, all the time and He is never late!

$$**********$$

Attending a Catholic school was my first introduction to God. Every Saturday I <u>had</u> to attend 'Confession' to tell the priest of any wrong doing I had committed that week. I remember never being able to think of anything to confess! I guess I felt that I had been a good little girl, so instead I used to make things up! So there I was in the Confession Box, lying to an Irish Priest because I couldn't think of anything I had done wrong! How ironic is that? As a note, I never attended a church methodically, per se, but as a youngish girl coming into teen hood, I did go and sometimes just sit in the Chapel. I believe I felt safe in there as it was quiet. Especially when there was nobody there; just pure silence and I loved the quietness and peacefulness it brought.

Perhaps I was being ministered to by God at that time but I just didn't know it. To this day, even though I have an outgoing personality and I LOVE people, I also crave spending a great deal of time on my own.

I'm actually much more introverted than people think. And therefore, time spent in silence and peace is so important to me. Also, I never even thought about it as God the Father, the Son and the Holy Spirit. It was more of a philosophy to me than anything real or tangible.

To say my stepfather was a troubled man is probably an understatement and one day whilst I was visiting grandad's he came into the house with my mum. I recall distinctly how solemn everyone appeared and the atmosphere in the room changed dramatically. My stepfather had just announced to everyone that he was dying of leukemia. I didn't know what leukemia was but I knew it must be something bad. Inside, I secretly breathed a sigh of relief and was glad that he would not be around for much longer. At last my pain and suffering would end I thought. However, over time, I began to feel guilty for having those thoughts.

As the weeks passed by my spirit was becoming more and more agitated. My thoughts and feelings concerning my stepfather's condition began to overwhelm me and eventually I decided to pluck up the courage and talk to our Priest. As I began to walk up the aisle of the Chapel, I thought that my legs would buckle but with each step I took I became more and more confident that I was doing the right thing. As I reached him, I asked if I could possibly speak with him in private. I have often wondered what the priest thought of this young girl approaching him that day and what she then started to impart. Towards the end of my statement I said, in my childlike explanatory manner,

'I think I could put up with him showing me things, if it meant he wouldn't die!'

The priest just listened to me and said nothing at the time. However, with hindsight I have often wondered if he did actually intervene. It is purely speculation to think he may have, but what I know for certain is that it wasn't speculation when I tell you that God did intervene and whether He used the priest or not to do it, I will probably never know. However, a short time later my mother and stepfather went their separate ways and I had been delivered once more! The abuse had ended. I distinctly remember feeling as though a huge load of bricks had been lifted from my shoulders. A child should not be walking around with a heavy load like that.

'We have escaped like a bird from the fowler's snare; the snare has been broken, and we have escaped.' Psalm 124:7

The irony of all of this is that my stepfather had not been diagnosed with anything, let alone leukemia! He had been lying to everyone and most of all to himself and his demise was imminent.

Over time my mother had other, very brief, relationships with men but none of them ever worked out and home life continued to be anything but perfect although I believe my mother worked hard and had so much mental anguish to recover from. My life was moving forward and I had already outgrown primary school. I had moved on to the high school. I was considered a very bright and clever child and I liked to entertain my peers! I had discovered that when I made people laugh, I got lots of attention and lots of friends! So I started to joke, all the way through high school, and, yes, I had lots of friends! School was like a retreat for me in the beginning and an escape from life. I was able to 'waltz' up and down the corridors, happy in the popular world I was creating for myself. However, there was one person that I didn't impress and no matter how hard I tried, my jokes did not make her laugh. Instead it made her jealous and envious. With jealousy and envy comes rage and over time she positioned herself as a ringleader and a bully. My entertaining days were cut short as she imposed her threats on everyone who paid attention to me or even spoke to me. The corridors started to become longer and narrower. My friends, like sheep, all turned their backs on me and rejection visited me once more.

Janie was another misfit in school, just like me! We soon found each other and started to hang out together. At the start, everyone poked fun and laughed at us but we stuck together and over time we were left alone. Janie had experienced tragedy in her short life also and therefore we connected immediately. She invited me to her home one day and thus began a friendship that would last for quite a few years. Janie was my first really close friend and I coveted and valued our relationship. Her grandad was also a great man and I got on well with him, just like I did with my own grandad. That's the thing about some grandparents, isn't it? They seem to know more and understand more and possess the wisdom that parents sometimes lack. They can be such an important bridge for a child, when communicating with parents is difficult. Going over to Janie's house every day after school soon became routine for me. Homework was forgotten. We had more important things to do such as listen for hours to 'George Michael' or 'Prince' records whilst crimping each other's hair! It was as if God had placed these twins together, just like David and Jonathan in the Bible. Through our friendship we sort of counselled each other and out of the tragic circumstances of our lives we could both live out our fantasies in our pretend girly world. Janie and I could escape the misery that the real world offered. It was during our times of playing records that I began to sing and in my mind there were no limitations and no one to say no to me. I dreamed that in the future I would fly to America to sign a big record deal. Perhaps I would meet my Prince, get married and live happily ever after! It was something I had carried forward, unwittingly from primary school. News soon spread that I was a really good singer and in order to gain favour with my classmates, I used to put on concerts for them. I would stand on my desk singing to a Smokey Robinson song or similar, gleaning adoration from my classmates. My friends would call to me and chant,

'Sing Ellie, SING!'

Of course I didn't want to disappoint my audience and in my subconscious I believe I equated singing with love. When I sang people loved ME and I fed off the attention.

I like to think that Janie got as much out of our friendship as I did and that she fondly looks back on those times. We were two kids who came from deeply troubling backgrounds where tragedy reigned and yet through the rejection of others somehow God had found a way to help us to escape and lean on one another.

I am forever grateful to God for Janie. She will always be an important part of my life where I can look back at that those certain times in my past and smile.

Chapter 3: I Must Get Out!

'...because God has said, "Never will I leave you; never will I forsake you." Hebrews 13:5

The years seemed to speed away from me and before long I was developing into a young woman and with most teenager girls going through those ever changing hormonal years, boys were becoming an interesting part of the landscape! I had met a young man in school, a year older than me; he had a colourful history to say the least. He was just a year older than I and he lived in a foster home. He told me he had spotted me walking past his house on my way home from school each day. He knew who I was but I had no idea who he was. Mark was always getting into trouble with the police and ultimately he did spent time in a remand centre. It was from this location he began to write to me at my home address. I didn't understand how he knew my postal address but I was bemused at receiving this attention and the first correspondence was a ten page letter. I confused his having a lot of spare time to dwell in his imaginations whilst locked up, with a belief that he was besotted with me! Although my mother had read the letter and expressed her view that she was not very pleased with the idea of me communicating with 'such a person,' I went against my better judgment and her advice and decided to embark on the relationship anyway. Making an informed decision for any teenager is a challenge but mine was based on poor examples of parenthood in this area and in particular men. Therefore I believe it is safe to say that apart from my mother's opinion, I was by and large allowed to make my own decisions without any opposition or indeed perfect guidelines. And I was about to discover with all decisions come consequences; good and bad.

Mark completed his time in the remand centre and then our relationship began.

As I mentioned previously my perception of males had been tainted from the beginning of my life, so therefore 'unseen qualities' had to present in order for me to embark on a relationship. Additionally, I firmly believe once you are out of alignment with God's Word from a young age, the prospect and probability of attracting harmful beings becomes a much higher potentiality. I see this now yet I was convinced that Mark was the perfect person for me. He had an adventurous, dangerous streak and I felt almost as if we were parallel souls. He was someone I could climb trees with; climb rocks with; have midnight adventures with out on the hills near my home with; swing on the swings with and laugh and enjoy our times together. However, Mark fed off my zest for life and started to drain it.

He, like other males I had known in my young life, did not know what the word 'no' meant. Mark forced me to have sexual relations with him; demanded it and, the acts that were forced upon me were debased, degrading and despicable. I would never have used the word, or even realised until years later that I was, in reality, being raped, physically, mentally and spiritually. I cannot begin to record those acts here. They belong in the darkness forever, but it is suffice to say that my character was even more damaged and influenced in a negative fashion and I felt like that helpless child of years before.

****

'Do not gloat over me, my enemy! Though I have fallen, I will rise. Though I sit in darkness, the LORD will be my light.' Micah 7:8

The only reason the relationship was interrupted was Mark was consigned to a prison sentence for an unrelated crime and eventually, through time and long after my encounter with him, Mark's actions took him to a whole new level of depravity and lawlessness and now he is currently serving a life sentence behind bars, for murder. How I have ruminated on the horror I was saved from, even at that time, when I didn't know of my Lord and

Saviour. God knew me before the foundations of the earth "I knew you before I formed you in your mother's womb" (Jeremiah 1:5) and it's because I know this that I can recognise how the enemy has tried, on copious occasions, to literally wipe me out! But the Lord has saved me, again and again as He knew the day would eventually arrive when I would turn to Him…..when I would KNOW He was ALWAYS with me.

****

Sexual abuse is a horrific crime against your body. And even though the crime is against your physical body, I believe the suffering is ingrained inside your soul and affects your whole life immensely. You develop feelings of debasement and contamination. Any woman who has experienced this will know what I am explaining…….and I pray that if you don't yet know Jesus Christ as your Lord and Saviour, that you turn to Him, because He is the only healer. He has the capacity and power to rid you of every feeling of unworthiness. He is the only One who can heal a broken and destitute heart and body. Only the Lord can cleanse you and make you feel new, redeemed and whole. And He does! Take it from me! I beseech you!

My encounter with Mark had planted seeds of anger, disillusionment and helplessness. Furthermore, it was around the same time I was dating him, that I had also experienced a sexual assault whilst walking home from school one day. I had been at a local college for interviews; preparing for my higher education and was happily walking home, preoccupied with the foretaste I had experienced of my immediate academic future, when it happened. Shocked, disorientated and in despair I made it home. The offences against my person seemed to be crowding in on me and when I look back now on those times it reminds me of something Jesus says in the Bible;

'Then it says, 'I will return to the house I left.' When it arrives, it finds the house unoccupied, swept clean and put in order. Then it goes and takes with it seven other spirits more wicked than itself, and they go in and live there. And the final condition of that

person is worse than the first. That is how it will be with this wicked generation.' Matthew 12: 44 & 45

I didn't know it at the time, as I hadn't ever studied the Bible, but in hindsight, it's almost as if I was meeting with all seven spirits at one time and that my condition, as well as the person harbouring them, was deteriorating. My body did not feel like my own property any more. It was as if anybody who wanted to accost me was able to; and whilst I was consumed in this state of darkness, I met Giuseppe.

I was walking a neighbour's dog on a very hot Good Friday, 1987. I had grown into what the world would consider a beautiful young woman. However, it seemed for me beauty had become a curse rather than a blessing. As I walked over the hills near my home, I noticed there was a group of young men hanging around one of the water lodges on top of the hills. The lodges were huge and many times people would swim in them, especially on hot days. I could see out of the corner of my eye that Giuseppe was watching me intently, but what I sensed was just that. He was watching me, not leering at me and it felt different. I knew one of the young men standing with the group as we had attended the same high school and I knew him to be a polite and decent young lad, so when his friend Giuseppe asked me if he could walk me home, I said he could. It was the first time I had ever really been asked something that felt so 'gentlemanly' and this was to be the beginning of my first legitimate relationship. Giuseppe would love me for who I was!

The issue with our relationship would be that I just couldn't figure out the concept of natural love and didn't know how to respond to it. It overwhelmed me at times. I had learned to protect my feelings; fears, insecurities and rejections. I had inadvertently built a wall around my mind and my heart and it was only when an individual got to really know me and I felt I could trust, in some way, that these emotions not only surfaced but would take on a whole new life of their own – it was as though I wasn't being controlled by the person so I had to be controlled by something.

It was some sort of mechanism. The unfortunate thing was, I was not equipped to deal with this mechanism. I now understand that the majority of the human race doesn't know how to either. Only Jesus knows. Giuseppe's love and care only exacerbated my inability to love back in a regular and ordinary way.

On one occasion we had a small disagreement and stopped speaking; a typical occurrence in any relationship when people are close. However, my method of dealing with this was not to try and work it out and communicate with each other. Oh, not at all! In those days my way to deal with any altercation was to take an overdose. I could not accept that level of rejection. Even though it was by no means, any level of rejection; it was just a silly argument. In my mind I thought I had lost the only good thing to ever happen to me. My heart ached with despair and to deal with any perceived, dejected ordeal, I had, heartbreakingly, learned this 'technique' from my mother.

****

One day in particular I was sent home from high school early with a migraine. I suffered terribly with migraines for years as a teenager. They were so bad that I would lose the use of half my body and would be unable to see properly. On this particular day when I reached my home I could not get inside. As my condition was becoming worse I called on our next door neighbour. The neighbour answered the door and as she saw it was me, instantly blurted out,

"Oh, your mum tried to kill herself. You'd better go to your grandad's"

I was devastated! Panic rushed through my veins; despair set into my soul. My head was throbbing and I tried to run as fast as I could to my grandad's. With each step I was starting to lose my vision, the daylight was piercing through my eyes, I needed the darkened room to alleviate my pain; but I couldn't think of that now I had to get to my grandad's. When I eventually reached his house he was grief stricken. I would have to wait another 24 hours to learn if my mother was alive or dead.

****

Therefore, suicidal ideation became a frequent visitor to me for many, many years. I would bluff myself that if times were not good during the day, I could plan a permanent way out in the evening.

Planning my death offered some form of reprieve and relief somehow. I felt a solace and that it was a goal to reach if I couldn't handle any daily stress. I came close on a few occasions to almost leaving this earth and I thank God to this day and every day for staving my hand. The enemy must have been extremely angry that I never fulfilled his mission for me because I have no doubt in my mind that it was one of his strategies. The enemy knew already that I was a daughter of the King; I just wasn't aware of it at that time. I would live to see many more days, some good and some bad and eventually with the power of the precious blood of Jesus and the promises He brings us, I would overcome my 'demons.'

****

If this book is in your hands right now and you have felt that the only escape is suicide; and you're wondering where is God in all of this, let me share something with you. After I was saved; after I gave my heart to the Lord, I had so many questions for Him. I DID ask Him! Where were you all those years that I had to suffer at the hands of others; where were you? Why did you let it happen? Why did you wait to be with me until I was 29 years old?" I asked Him time and time again but it wasn't until I was willing to sit and actually listen for His answers, that I realised there is a plan. And that our Mighty God knows exactly what He is doing. He is the Alpha and the Omega; He knows the beginning from the end! Even though to me, and to you, as you read this book, it looked as though I was on a constant road to destruction; that the enemy was truly in control of every aspect of my life, in reality, I was, from the day I was born, on the road to restoration, renewal and revival! The enemy knew that inside of me was a warrior woman who would want to commit to working for the Kingdom; working for her Lord, for eternity! God already had the Victory! And so did I! I just didn't know it yet!

At this juncture I want to talk a little about salvation and healing and what it means to me. Jesus died on the Cross for MY sins and in order for me to have eternal life, with Him, in heaven. It actually blows my mind, every day! For a good number of years, AFTER I was saved, I couldn't come to terms with it. I was filled with the Spirit; I had visions; I had words of knowledge; God still used me. Yet it took years of healing for me to accept, that in His eyes, I wasn't worthless; I was saved! I had very deep-seated issues with rejection and worthlessness and it has taken literally years. As I write this, I know

I am healed, although I do 'take captive' instantly, any silly thoughts that come into my head.   I'm actually at the stage now where I can think,

'It doesn't really matter who 'rejects' me, because God never will.'

Although, I do have situations where I still have to remember exactly who I am in the world and exactly who I am in Christ! I'm far from perfect and we are always growing and learning. Only Jesus is perfect. There was a time; I thought He would reject me. That wasn't anything God did, just my deep-seated and tragic, learned behaviour.   When you've had as many hard knocks as I have had, it's not really any wonder is it? BUT GOD IS MY REDEEMER. Instead of existing; surviving; I now FLOAT, LIVE and OVERCOME! Because of Him! Hallelujah!

'The LORD Almighty has sworn, "Surely, as I have planned, so it will be, and as I have purposed, so it will happen.' Isaiah 14:24

I believe that God has given each and every one of us freewill and I also understand that there are many people out there who believe that Christians brainwash their children by sending them to church and force-feeding them a diet of 'hell, fire and damnation' if they do anything deemed as sinful. In a world that offers nothing but violence, disrespect, disharmony, and greed; a world without boundaries; I believe that church offers children the opportunity to experience relationships with their peers, outside of the classroom, teaching them how to overcome different situations in a calm, controlled environment through communication and prayer; where love and, not violence, is the rule.

****

A further issue I had to contend with and be delivered from when I was saved was my involvement and experience with the occult. When one begins to dabble in the occult it can have a devastating effect on their children; especially when they are young. It can rob a child of security and safety. My mother chose to look to the occult for answers to her life issues. By the time I was leaving 'friends' I had been taught how to read tarot cards and regularly partook of the Ouija boards. When I look back at that time, I thank God for rescuing me again. However, it would take a lot more prayer and deliverance after I was saved for that root to be completely pulled out.

Chapter 4: Decisions

'Anyone who does not provide for their relatives, and especially for their own household, has denied the faith and is worse than an unbeliever' .Tim 5:8

Because of the trauma caused by the sexual assault, coming back from my college interviews, I decided not to go to that college. Understandably, I was scared of being attacked again and anxious of ever having to walk through that area of town again. But I was making these incorrect choices through the spirit of fear. With the knowledge of God's Word, I can look back on this time now and understand these things bathed in His light and wisdom.

****

The enemy is so subtle in his attempts to manoeuvre people and situations into our lives and to create chaos and unhappiness for all involved. It keeps our focus not on God but on the situations and we become self-absorbed and only interested in what the world can offer us. Therefore, if you're not even aware of God; His existence and love for you, then you're not aware of the enemy either; his existence and his villainous hatred for you. Hence, when one is living a life with many traumatic and consistent events, one tends to fixate on the pain and the problems. That is a dream to the enemy, as he knows that when you are intrinsically self-absorbed you're next step to improving your mental, emotional or physical state is less disinclined.

Nowadays, as my daughter will testify, I live by the theory of 'Choices; Decisions; Consequences'. I teach my daughter this and also that for every problem or issue we face, there IS a solution. Primarily and most essential, is prayer and the power of prayer. If I had possessed this knowledge in my younger years, I believe my journey would have been markedly changed!

****

That year was one of *the* defining moments in my life for me. I was becoming more and more difficult to live with and my mother had a very delicate disposition. Our personalities clashed! It was becoming more and more evident that we could not live with each other, so she made a decision unknown to me. One day she put all my clothes in supermarket plastic bags and dropped them off at the jewelry shop where I was employed. She had literally kicked me out of the home and I had nowhere to go! I do remember it was because I hadn't washed some pots and pans and maybe it was the last straw for her.

I was in shock and felt humiliated in front of colleagues; abandoned by my own mother. I was so ashamed and tried to cover up and pretended I had to take the clothes to someone's house. I rang Giuseppe and was able to stay at his house, in secret, for two nights. He didn't reside in a very functional home either, so there was no prospect of me staying there permanently. He had a lot of family members; old and young, it was impossible and because of that, I sadly ended up squatting for weeks in a rat-infested house near to where Giuseppe lived. I struggled to get washed and fed and because of my inability to present myself in a fashion required by the shop, ultimately I lost my job. They didn't ask me to leave; I left of my own accord. There was a concrete and consolidated shame lying upon my shoulders and I felt unworthy and embarrassed to be there. I had no money, no home and no family. I was totally alone. I think back to that time, and as a mother I think of my own daughter. How would I have reacted to her 'attitude?' I like to think that no matter what trials or tribulations we go through as a mother and daughter I will never close the door on her, ever.

****

Living in that ramshackle terraced house; my home; the squat, was safer than being on the streets. My most memorable recall is of the rats that would come up to me as I slept on an old mattress that must have been used by someone else previously. Do you know? I didn't fear them, at all. I didn't fear the darkness. It was dark all the time because of the wood nailed to the window frames. At that time, I just carried shame. The future wasn't even an issue. I still had this optimism inside me that I was going to have a good life; it was as though I knew, in my heart, that 'someone' was with me. I know it was God. I know now; I just didn't know then. I've always had an ability to be happy on the outside no matter what is going on within me. One day I was walking down the street and the local window cleaner saw me. I had known him for all of my life and he shouted out 'Hey, Smiler!' I shouted back 'Good morning!' and I remember beaming. I remembered that I am a smiler; and smiling is better than crying! It's funny, but I remember the next step I took and I felt all warm inside. Something was telling me; this 16 year old scrawny kid; that I was going to be ok. The window cleaner gave me a five pound note. I haven't a clue why!! And I went and bought some cereal and ate it. It was DELICIOUS! Even to this day, it's the little things I appreciate and thank God for every day; heat in my beautiful but simple apartment; food in the cupboards; a small vase of flowers; a plant that I'm watering and nurturing; these are the things that make me a 'smiler'.

****

One day, as if by chance, (more like a God-incidence!) I met a girl I had known from school. Her face said it all when she saw me and she gave me a hug. I certainly didn't look like the girl from school! She offered for me to stay with her in her small cramped bedsit. I felt like I had been transported to a millionaire's mansion! I had a hot shower and the water felt so good and then she made me a scrumptious and gratifying meal and for the first time in months I had a soft warm bed to sleep in. My life had turned another corner and God had found a way again. I will be forever grateful to my friend from school. She is in my prayers each night. I don't know if she knows it but she saved my life and she allowed me to stay with her until I was able to get on my feet. I had survived!

'Then they cried to the LORD in their trouble, and he saved them from their distress.' Psalm 107:13

Soon after, I was able to get a job in a local restaurant and in turn and through time was able to afford my very own bedsit, my first home! I could not afford to go to college now which was so upsetting as I had big dreams and I was eager to study. I had a mind hungry for knowledge, but this part of me was now stunted by my circumstances. This frustrated me further as I was smart and eager to work at academia. Like everyone I had dreams and ambitions to have a great career and here I was without any form of family, living in a bedsit and working in a restaurant at sixteen! I still love to study and learn even now. We should never stop learning! Because of my love of sports and fitness I decided to train as an aerobics instructor instead as I could fit this around my job. I had always been good at sport and loved long distance running, so I gravitated towards this area. For the next couple of years I lived totally dedicated to my job in fitness but regrettably, because of my resentment of the fact I was unable to pursue my innate desires to better myself, I developed a 'couldn't care less' attitude. I had a deep adventurous streak as well as any other academic desires and I was still turning to read the tarot cards for guidance in my life. One day while in work I was really hungry and decided to help myself to some raspberries and whipped cream without paying for them. I sneaked into the toilets to eat them but unfortunately I got caught and I lost my job, instantly. I have repented of this! However, that week I had learned of an available role for an assistant in a top hotel in the Lake District. This was much further north than where I lived and the Lake District is one of the most spectacularly beautiful places in England! I was young, almost nineteen years old now and free, so it felt like an adventure! Indeed, it would take me far, far away from my northern town and in my mind, from all the angst and past misgivings, to one of the most stunning areas in England. I arrived by train and bus with as much luggage as I could bring. I adapted well to the job and loved working in the hotel. I met visitors from all over the world and greetings and messages would be left at the reception in envelopes for me, that if ever the 'happy, smiling, Lancashire lass' was in Canada, or Tokyo, or France; anywhere and everywhere, that I had to look them up! Additionally, I had time to soak up and appreciate the beauty all around. The magnificence of the mountains and the way they looked like velvet permeated my every pore and I absorbed every minute of spare time to run around the lakes and through the woods and up the hills and mountains. It was heaven to me! I guess it was rooted in me from the times I had spent with my grandad and I was immersed in the breathtaking beauty of my new, calm and stable environment. It was one of the few times in my young adult life that I had felt true happiness and I made a couple of life-long friends whilst I was there. I did miss the love Giuseppe showed me though and I had tried to keep in touch with him. Then one day I was returning from a run and as I got back to my accommodation a car drove up to the main door.

"That man looks just like Giuseppe", I thought to myself as I entered the doorway to shower and get ready for my next work shift. I retraced my steps back again and took another closer look. It was Giuseppe! I immediately forgot my shift and ran towards him and straight into his arms. He had driven

all the way up to the Lake District to find me! I couldn't believe it! I hadn't believed he would be missing me so much and he wanted to take me back to our hometown. In hindsight, this was to suit his own needs, but I perceived it to be because he loved me so much. When one is desperate to be loved and someone shows just a portion of what feels like love, it causes wrong decisions to be made. I thought we could be together forever and I felt that he would do anything for me following that gesture so I decided to throw caution to the wind! I decided to move back to our hometown with Giuseppe; we would get married, have lots of babies and live happily ever after! So I did. I moved back home with Giuseppe that very week……

As I looked across to the driver's side of the car and watched Giuseppe intently I can honestly say at that moment, I could see my future with him. I was so desperate to belong to someone in the right way, someone who would love me for who I was and someone I could love safely. I have a great capacity for love. I desire to love the 'unlovely, the abandoned and forlorn.' However, the only 'person' I believed that could fulfill true love in my life would be a baby. Something of my very own, to treasure and something that no-one could harm or take away from me. So as I looked at Giuseppe, I started to imagine our child; a little boy with dark hair and the bluest of eyes. I could see him in my mind and I already had a name for him; a Biblical name. I don't know why it had to be Biblical but I remember it was important to me!

Giuseppe also wanted children and particularly a boy. He couldn't wait for an 'Italian' son to carry on the family name and traditions. I was super excited and as soon as I knew I was pregnant I was in love, bubbling over with excitement. I ran to Giuseppe with the good news! However, within days things started to change. He became very distant and the dream started to fade like a burning spitfire in front of my eyes. Upon our return from the Lake District, I had moved into Giuseppe's newly bought home. At first it was wonderful but then following the news of my pregnancy he started to bring other women back to the house after his nights out. Abandoned and pregnant I could only go to the bedroom and cry my heart out as I realised that the dream of the perfect home and family was gone. I questioned myself of course, 'What is going on? How could this happen?' Again I had no answer, but Giuseppe did. He didn't want to provide for me and wanted me out. He admitted he couldn't cope with the responsibility. I frantically searched my mind, 'Where could I go?' Can you imagine being in this situation again; about to become homeless and now carrying a child! You may ask why I didn't go to my grandfather but I wanted to avoid worrying him and he was already very disappointed that I was pregnant and unmarried. I couldn't bear for him to have this to be concerned about now. I had a little money, so I knew I would be able to sort something out accommodation wise for a short while. When I had left the hotel in the Lake District they owed me a lump sum and at my request I asked them to deposit it in Giuseppe's account as I didn't have one and had always been paid cash. In those days wages could still be paid on a weekly cash basis so I hadn't ever needed an account. As far as I was concerned, we both needed the money and particularly now that we had a baby on the way; I had no reason to distrust Giuseppe. I had searched the newspapers and found a women's hostel. I fitted the criteria needed to stay there. So there I was, standing in a doorway once more with bags full of clothes, not only myself rejected this time, but my baby as well and by his own father. I turned around and asked Giuseppe for my hard earned money that was in his account. I will never forget (although I have forgiven) he went back into the house and returned with ten pound coins and placed them in my hand. I was devastated and appalled! This was all that his baby meant to him. I found out afterwards, that the very same day I had left; the day he literally threw out his child and mother of his child, he had gone out to a dog shelter and bought a puppy!

Many, many years later, I met up with Giuseppe and he asked me a question. He asked 'Why have you forgiven me so easily?' I was able to say, 'Because I have Jesus in my heart and unforgiveness is the most bitter of roots to have in your body. Once I knew Jesus, I was able to forgive all of your actions because I see you as Jesus sees you'.

****

The homeless shelter for women was very strict. The layers of pain I felt being left alone, isolated and pregnant I cannot accurately describe to you. I thought that many parts of my life up until this point had been lousy but this was the worst. As an expectant mother I yearned for all the things that any first time mother wants; not so much for herself but for her unborn baby. I wanted my baby to be loved and accepted by all; with a cosy home and a nursery with lots of toys and I dreamed of one day marrying and having a family unit. But to be candid and in hindsight, even though I reasoned it was what I wanted on a couple of occasions, as I look back, in my heart it wasn't what I truly desired. I was, in truth, diffident of the 'ideal family' situation; suspicious and intimidated by my fear of failure. I wanted the perception of the 'ideal family' and would have settled and grabbed for whatever I could but that is neither God's way nor will. I'm so glad I didn't get married as it seems I would probably have been divorced more than once and I would not have been true to myself! Before I was saved, I felt marriage was just a piece of paper and actually believed it was a wrong thing for anyone to do. It wasn't until I was saved and knew God, that I then realised marriage was and is a God ordained covenant between a man and woman.

****

I have had two marriage proposals in my life; one of which I knew was a 'no way' response and the other I agreed to but then I used to have hot sweats and wake up petrified of being committed to someone forever! He also was 'ecstatic' (his words) at the thought of us being married, then after a week he panicked too! Now, I wish to make this very important statement – I do not condone having sex outside of marriage, or having children out of wedlock. However, if you do not know God and you are not brought up in a Christian household, like me, it's left to the secular world to mould your views and we know who the secular world belongs to, don't we?

My beliefs now are formed by my relationship with God and what His Word says. I had both of my children before I was saved and both were born out of wedlock. Yet Father God in His mercy and grace has enabled them to have the life I did not. Both were saved from a young age and my daughter has been in church and brought up in a Christian household since she was born.

One of the first scriptures I ever read and knew was *'For your creator will be your husband......'* And He truly meant it! After 14 years I am still not married and even though earlier in my saved years I had a couple of wobbles, I have been faithful to God. I now feel for the first time in my life that I am ready to be married and I do want to be married. I wish to partake in that ministry of marriage; I do want to be someone's helpmate. But you know, God has a plan and if it happens, it happens and if it doesn't, it doesn't.

I am so in love with Jesus, with my beautiful journey and this plan He has for me, that I feel complete peace with it all. Plus, I have a very happy home life with my daughter and right now, that's what works for us. I have a lot of freedom and I believe God is constantly taking me to another level in Him. It's all preparation isn't it? For here and for Heaven.

'For your Maker is your husband-- the LORD Almighty is his name-- the Holy One of Israel is your Redeemer; he is called the God of all the earth' .Isaiah 54:5

Chapter 5: Something to Cling To

'Turn, LORD, and deliver me; save me because of your unfailing love.' Psalm' 6:4

One simple but pleasant memory I have about the shelter is that I had been given a little radio and I used to listen to it as I fell asleep at night. I would talk to my baby and stroke my tummy and tell the baby what each song meant to me as it came on. I don't even remember which station it was but it used to play tracks from the 70's and 80's. Nowadays they would seem old but it was only the summer of 1991 and they were perfect.

One song in particular I loved was the song *'All over the world'* by the Electric Light Orchestra. It would constantly be playing and I knew every word.

In the midst of all the mess I found myself in; the trauma and the rejection, I used to sing to my baby and make plans that we would travel all over the world someday. Unbelievably this was like a prophetic word being spoken over our lives because nowadays I spend most of my life literally travelling all over the world! And I know my son does also. I still listen to that song to this very day; it makes me smile and I remember those dreams I had back then.

I was in love with the baby I was carrying and with the wonderful gift that God was giving me. I never gave God a second thought, but now I know it was Him allowing me to bring this precious child into the world. I may have had extreme hardship around me but it was like I had two hearts inside of me beating as one and I was responsible for both! One night whilst sitting in my room, I made a decision. Nothing would ever come between me and my baby ever! I would do everything within my power to protect him and drench him in love. I had enough love for both of us. I would find work, I would provide a home and he would love his life!

It was December 28th, 1991 and the pains started gradually. I knew the moment had arrived, and my labour day was imminent! After an incredible fifteen and a half hours, I gave birth to Samuel, my 7lb 8oz baby boy! I already knew what I was going to call him. The name Samuel derives from the Hebrew name Shemu'el, which has two meanings, 'Name of God' or 'God has heard.' At this time, as I write, I realise the latter was the most appropriate. He was perfect! Love is not the word to describe it; as if it isn't a big enough word to use! It was an unbelievable power of love that I felt; total immersion, where everything else in the world just melted away. I was only 20 years old and I was extremely street wise and confident in my abilities to look after Samuel. Looking back, as I stared into the beautiful blue eyes of my newborn son, I knew deep within my heart that God had heard my cries.

Although I was what many consider 'too young to be a mother' at only twenty years old, and now I totally agree, I was determined to make our lives very different from what I had experienced personally in my own life. If I had learned anything, it was how not to treat another human being. Samuel was all mine and all I wanted was to pour out all the love that was locked inside of me onto Samuel. I would defend him forever.

At approximately the same time that I had been in hospital with Samuel, there had been a few incidents where babies had been snatched from their mothers in hospitals. These news incidents played on my mind, as they would for any good mother. I was apprehensive at the possibility of a security lapse at our hospital and therefore I decided that the best thing would be to keep Samuel with me at all times. The majority of the staff were very kind and understanding although there was one particular Ward Sister who was from the 'old school!' She was feared, I believe, by her peers, patients, and doctors! She seemed detached from her work, as though her heart was not in it. Perhaps she was working in the wrong department. To me, she did not display a maternal bone in her body.

I understand that routine is important for nursing staff. I totally accept that. However, with the alerts and abductions at other hospitals, I was really only seeking a little understanding. It was shower time for me but I did not wish to leave Samuel on his own in my room, as the queue was particularly long and waiting in line would have meant that I would have been away from Samuel. This was unacceptable for me. To leave him for any period of time was a 'no, no' but for an extended period, with no nursing staff available to watch over him, it developed into a definite 'NO!'

Therefore, I decided the optimal decision would be to take him with me into the shower room. I could do this by wheeling his plastic hospital cot into the bathroom. The Ward Sister saw me going towards the shower, wheeling the small plastic cot down the corridor. Immediately she ordered me to take Samuel back to our room. Unfortunately for her, she did not know that I possessed a very strong will and I refused to leave him on his own. I couldn't fathom why she refused to support my reasons for wanting to keep my baby safe.

'That's fine, I won't bathe then,' I retorted.

Unfortunately the situation intensified and escalated. Like an emotional tug of war. Even then, as a young woman I could see that this woman had only her dictatorial identity to cling on to and that the issue itself wasn't the issue! She just needed to be in control. Something I could quite easily understand years later. However, the experience made me conscious of the depth of feelings I had for this little child and the responsibility that it carried.

Up until now my life had been one of total rejection! I resolved that no-one in this world either wanted to help or support me and my deep seated insecurities were only compounded further by this incident. The fact that people had always micromanaged me or wanted to exert control over my life had left me damaged. This episode had far reaching effects within me. It only served to exacerbate my need to control everything in the years to come. Again my freewill had been tampered with and it was just one circumstance too many. With the passing of time it became more and more necessary for me to protect my feelings and become the controller and not the device.

The rest of my time in hospital passed off without incident and the day had arrived when I would finally be able to take Samuel home. I was excited about this as by now I had moved out of the shelter and into our little two bedroomed terraced home. Of course it wasn't very sumptuous or regal but it was totally ample for both of us. It was the new start that Samuel and I both needed and I proceeded to make a beautiful home for us.

At first I relished being in my own space and being able to make my own decisions without being judged. I loved being a first time mummy but I was alone and isolated somewhat and this, through time, would give way to depression. Although I was very young and alone with a new baby, I was able to cope to a certain extent. However, the nights grew longer and lonelier. There was no 'dad' to support us and even though my mother did help with Samuel and my grandfather adored him, the detachment I was feeling, combined with the rejection I had suffered personally throughout the years, caused me to become more and more anxious.

Inadvertently, I was the one putting more and more pressure on myself. I cannot pinpoint a definite time or what the catalyst was for the postnatal depression but I had all the standard emotions and symptoms that many new mum's have; insomnia, panic attacks, not eating and over anxious. What I do know is that after a while these feelings gave way to actual fear. My soul was gripped by it and my entire being began to slip deeper and deeper, in abysmal rhythmic waves, into the darkness. At first I was petrified that someone would steal Samuel, abuse him or perhaps he would be harmed by breathing in polluted air. After a while I would start to experience panic or anxiety attacks, whilst shopping for instance. It was terrible and it had got to the point it was affecting my ability to function and enjoy daily life with my son. My dream was becoming a nightmare. Prison bars had risen up around me and I didn't know how to get out. Eventually, my condition was noticed and a couple of my friends persuaded me to seek medical attention.

The doctor diagnosed me with postnatal depression. Whilst no one really wants to have a diagnosis, this in itself released me. I knew now I was not dying or going mad but I was experiencing something that about 85 percent of women experience at some point in their lives. I was reassured that I didn't need to be afraid anymore. Even though I was heedless of God's intervention I now know He was in that process and had begun a new thing deep within me. The blackness was turning a lighter shade of grey and His light was starting to break through. It would take some more time but I had, I believed, turned a corner…….

'See, I am doing a new thing! Now it springs up; do you not perceive it? I am making a way in the wilderness and streams in the wasteland' Isaiah 43:19

****

It is said that time is a healer and I believe this. Nonetheless, some situations can be wedged within and it takes more than time to heal and this can still continue to affect your 'decision making' processes for many years to come; in fact, even after you have accepted Jesus as your Lord and Saviour. Those months in the women's shelter may have been difficult but they gave me a roof over my head and protection. As I look back I will always be forever grateful to God that I had a place where I was free from the persecution that I had experienced at the hand of men and that I was with other women. I don't wish to sound 'anti-men' but for me that was extremely important at that time. It enabled me to have time with myself during my pregnancy and have peace. As referred to earlier, I had the company of other women and these women were also homeless generating a sort of understanding and bond between us. I would be lying if I said that shelter life was not difficult and not ideal; it was extremely difficult at times. Through it all, however, as I look back I know that God had His hand on both of us, my baby and I, every second of every day.

The decisions that we make in life, either big, or what we perceive to be inconsequential, are inordinately crucial because they affect our journey. If we make the 'right' or 'wrong' decisions then we reap the harvest of this; good or bad. This is why it is vital to consult with Jesus about everything. This is also true whenever other's make decisions on your behalf. I know because I have lived it! However, some people struggle when they come into the Kingdom to hand everything over to Jesus and subjectively, I believe that it's because of the distrust created by other's making decisions on their behalf.

When I became saved the hardest procedure was learning to trust a 'Father' as my experiences of a 'father' per se, hadn't been anything like my Father in Heaven. What I can tell you is when you maneuver through this transitional period, allowing Jesus to freely make the decisions on your behalf you can have certainty that it is the right one. 'How do I know?' I hear you ask. How do I really know it is Jesus? For the reason that Jesus told His disciples something very important;

'I have told you these things, so that in me you may have peace. In this world you will have trouble. But take heart! I have overcome the world.' John 16:33

After prayer and meditation over the Word of God, you know you are not only in the right position but you are aligned with His Word and ready to receive His peace, it's as simple as that!

****

My first encounter with born-again Christians was a young couple who were in the house attached to mine. They used to welcome me in for a drink or snack frequently and Sam and myself would have tea and chat about everyday things. I didn't know they were Christians at the time but I knew they were friendly people and invited me to a couple of events in their home. I attended, not because I didn't want to offend them, but because I wanted to be a part of whatever they were doing. There was something about this little family that intrigued me. Therefore, something had started to change……… But, I was totally unaware of exactly what it was!

Many years later, after I was saved, I met them by chance at a church event. They were so happy to see me and told me that they were always praying for me and Samuel. They were praying specifically for my salvation and nine years later I gave my heart to Jesus and so did Samuel! It never ceases to amaze me how from the faith of a mustard seed can one person's life be changed, dramatically and for eternity! God has purposes and plans for our lives but we tend to stray and make bad choices and decisions which knock things off course profoundly! Yet, through the consistent prayers and love of the saints, God is preparing and maneuvering behind the scenes. Never give up praying because its Gods will that every soul be saved, that none should perish. It was a wonderful day for that family to know that their prayer had caused me and my son, and eventually my daughter, to live in eternity. Not in Hell…..but in Heaven!

Returning back to the time when we were neighbours and considering I had another nine years to go before my salvation, I often look back and think 'Oh why didn't I hear in my heart from God then? Why didn't I make the decision for Him then instead of relying on myself?' Yet the wonderful denouement is, no matter what choices we make, once we accept Jesus as our Lord and Saviour, He can access all of those things in the past and turn them all around for HIS GLORY.

He is the God of yesterday, today and tomorrow and He will use it all to heal us and others...

'And we know that in all things God works for the good of those who love him, who have been called according to his purpose'. Romans 8:28

Chapter 6: Goodbye My Friend

'But I am hard-pressed from both directions, having the desire to depart and be with Christ, for that is very much better; yet to remain on in the flesh is more necessary for your sake''
Philippians 1:23-24

Samuel's father never did connect to Samuel. I would go alternately from feeling sadness to agonising heartbreak, but this was more for my son than myself. When you are a person with a magnitude of love inside of you for another human being, particularly a child you have birthed, it's hard to perceive how another parent cannot find that devotion inside of them and you hurt for the child. Anyone who is a parent knows this feeling; the love you have for your own is immeasurable and indescribable. This is what astounds me now, as I consider that God loves any one of us more than any love we can possibly grasp! Wow!

Despite all of these feelings of hurt I felt for Samuel, feeling he was rejected by his daddy and the depressive illness I was enduring, Samuel and I had a peaceful, balanced life together and adapting to life as a mother was far from difficult for me. The saying many use when they completely adore another 'He or She is my life!' I can totally accept. Samuel truly was my life! Because of my close bond with my grandfather, we would spend as much time as possible with him and I knew he would be a great paternal influence for Samuel. They were immensely joyous times and I will treasure them always. The thing about memories is nobody can ever steal the ones you choose to keep.

My grandfather was getting on in years and he had suffered from angina for a period of ten years. Around this time he had been experiencing a great deal of pain which didn't seem to diminish even with his medications. I honestly believed he would be around, for me, forever. I couldn't ever comprehend I would lose him. A momentous comment he made one day had me questioning his well-being and mortality.

"I hope I live long enough to see Samuel walk"

I was stunned and didn't really want to think about it. I brushed it off to the side and tried to forget he had said it. I wanted to believe that we would always be able to spend time together with little Sam and that of course he would be around to see Samuel take his first steps.

Now, as a woman in her forties, I can remember with compassion and love many conversations we had. He used to tell me of his times in the Second World War and the suffering he not only endured, but saw. He had escaped a prisoner-of-war camp and had travelled by foot, on his own, to Austria, where some nuns had taken him in and cared for him. He weighed a mere six stones and I recall part of his survival had been when he had only some sugar to eat. I am sad that I cannot remember more about his story as I try my utmost to share with my daughter. To me he was and, always will be, a hero for England. He kept some very beautiful walnut rosary beads that had been pressed into his hands by one of the nuns. He kept them very safe. I imagine when he touched them they reminded him not only of horror and pain, but of the compassion, love and safety he had felt when the nuns took him in.

It was during these conversations we had, that he would affirm his disillusionment with the world and how he was tired; not just at the world but within himself and I now see that the intensity of his heart condition and the depth of his weariness were kept hidden from me. He wouldn't have wanted me to worry. I did used to tell him "I don't know what I would do if I didn't have you Grandad".

****

Several weeks later, my grandfather phoned me at my home one evening, around 8.30pm, to inform me that he was going into hospital that very night, under his doctor's recommendation, for observation. He had actually had a small heart attack earlier in the day but he hadn't wanted to give me cause for concern so I don't think he would have even mentioned it if he wasn't having to be admitted to the hospital for more tests.   Of course I was quite perturbed but was hesitant to give him any further distress so I thanked him in a positive tone for letting me know and asked him to keep me informed of what was happening. I told Him 'I love you more than the world' and I'll never forget his words returned to me,

"I love you too; you and Sam. Don't worry; I love you darling."

I put the phone down, not knowing that would be the last time I ever heard the voice of my best friend; my rock; my grandfather.

My cherished Grandad died at 5am the next morning and to say I was absolutely inconsolable and heartbroken would be an understatement. I can remember the moments just before my mother broke the news. As soon as I heard the knock at the door, I instantly discerned in my heart that it wasn't good news. However, it did not lessen the blow of the shock on hearing it;

"Don't say it; don't say the words," I screamed at her; my face soaked with tears. I felt, as soon as the words were spoken out loud, that I would crumble. I needed to prepare somehow, but how can you ever prepare for the inevitable; when it's the worst news that you're about to hear?

I put my hands over my ears to try and escape the words; the pain. It was one of the darkest times in my life. My ally; my best friend was gone. Oh, how I loved that gentle, compassionate man. Even as I write these words over twenty years later, my heart remembers the ache. But I can thank God for circumstances that He maneuvered because my grandfather's main wish; main prayer even, was granted.

Samuel started to walk at 10 months and within months of Samuel walking my adorable grandfather was gone. He had died, but not before he had seen Sam walking. There was a specific country walk we would take. Before we hit the hills, there was a long cobbled path we would walk; me with Samuel in a baby carrier on my chest and grandad at my side. As far as I am concerned, God had already seen all three of us walking up that long path to the hills. A place we loved! And it was that path that my grandfather walked, whilst holding hands with a little boy that toddled along beside him. A memory I hold in my heart and mind for all eternity. I consider it such a blessing that God granted James Anthony Aspin to be my grandfather. I'll never forget his twinkly, piercing blue eyes and jet black thick hair. His big hands that created so much; hands that held a granddaughter close when she needed a hug; hands that produced so many amazing products through his carpentry skills; hands that wrote poetry with beautiful calligraphy. I have so many letters I have saved that he wrote whenever I was travelling somewhere. They are kept safe in an old battered suitcase I keep with other sentimental cards, letters and items. He will always be in my heart.

****

The funeral was equally difficult but not as much as the chasm that had been created by his passing. *"Goodbye, my friend"* I said to myself. *"I'll always love you"*.

An era was over.

****

Living as a single parent was extremely difficult but the times I had being with Samuel were treasured times and I didn't waste any moments to be with him. There was nothing like putting him in his little carry pouch and climbing the hills I loved to ramble over, with him close to my chest. I loved feeding him and tickling him. Making him giggle made life worth living and it was my joy in him that directed me towards hope and to live again. My love for Sam spilled over to other children and I knew then that I wanted to return to college and study nursery nursing.

After the passing of my grandfather I was feeling a void and it caused a loneliness that made me yearn for some love just for me; a partner; a love interest; a father for Samuel. Again I dwelled upon the idea of getting married and having lots more children.

One night, I decided to join some friends for a 'girl's night out'. It had been a while since I had socialised. With the recent episodes of loss and being a busy single parent I had neither the inclination nor the spare money. So when a close friend asked me to join a group of our mutual friends, I decided to meet up with them at a local bar and have a night out. One of my friends, Elisha, was dating a guy who seemed to be what one would refer to as 'gangster'. Now, when I say 'gangster' I don't mean a local street gang member. I mean a more 'heavy duty' type. Brandon seemed to make Elisha happy and I was happy for her but I was naïve and oblivious to many of the unscrupulous events going on around her and later, myself. Brandon had a close friend called Steve. He was an older, more mature man. We were introduced very briefly and then I continued chatting with the other girls, not really giving any of Brandon's group of friends a second thought; I was just being polite. The rest of evening was uneventful and went well. I was tired, eager to get home and see my son and cosy up in bed.

It was a few weeks after that night out, in the late Autumn time, when one evening my phone rang and I answered to the huskiest, deepest male voice on the other end instantly asking,

"Could I possibly spend a whole evening looking into those eyes?"

I was a little startled and didn't recognise who it was. He continued to explain that he was Brandon's friend and that we had met previously within a mutual group of friends. I then realised who it was. It was Steve but I hadn't really given him a second thought and barely recalled our brief introduction. I had rarely dated anyone since Samuel's birth. I just wasn't interested in that sort of commitment. However, as I previously wrote, at that particular time I had thought of meeting someone special and for Samuel to have a father figure. Therefore, not only was I slightly taken aback, I was also easily charmed and flattered by Steve's invitation. Should I consider? Should I give it a miss? Could I be bothered? But what if he was a really nice man? I couldn't turn him down could I?

Therefore I agreed, tentatively, to a date with Steve on none other than Halloween! It soon arose that Steve was one of the most well-known high level criminals in the area and was involved in a national drugs scandal at one time through which he was imprisoned for many years. I was not aware of this at the time. However, what I noticed habitually on our nights out was his treatment by others. It was as though he was a god! People regarded him with such high esteem and respect, almost as though he was royalty. In fact, when I was with him, I was looked upon with the same respect and it made me feel important. People would whisper as we entered venues, "that's so and so and that's his woman". I felt for the first time the centre of attention in someone's world; even though it was actually Steve's world, but I liked it. The very sad thing is I equated the whole attention and respect position with love. I wanted to be loved so desperately that I thought this was it. I thought this was love. I relished my new status. However, it was a red herring. Steve didn't really care for me at all in the way I believed he did and I was a 'side dish' to be admired by all and paraded before many.

Initially, our dates were just wining and dining and I enjoyed that. There wasn't an immediate commitment involved and after a while and a few intuitions, I had convinced myself it was just for a season. However, eventually my feelings did develop for him and I definitely felt that I wanted to be with him; in fact I thought I needed him. He was a father figure for sure. He was 25 years older than me and in his late forties. However, things were not what they seemed. I discovered that Steve was a married man. At first it bothered me but he was so persuasive and convincing in his explanations of his life at home, that I became almost immune to any sensitivity because the 'Steve says' syndrome ruled my thinking. I even accepted his ridiculous statement that it was normal for a man to love more than one woman! Because he would spend time with Samuel and I at home and play with Samuel as though he was a loving father, I decided to block out all the dubious and disputable thoughts about Steve, particularly that he had a wife. I was a young, troubled woman and had always been able to delete anything from my mind that could hurt me or did hurt me so even though I am sad at the cruelty and disregard shown for Steve's wife, at that time, I truly didn't know any better. I understand the scripture so well "Forgive them Lord for they know not what they do". When you live your life without Jesus; without being Spirit-filled, you are living a worldly life. It's a life without any accountability. As a believer, you know you are accountable to God, before you're accountable to any person. Plus, I believe a worldly existence is the most self-focused existence. You are only ever really accountable to yourself and even if living what is seen as a good, honest life, without being spirit-filled, you will never see others, through God's eyes, or love others, with the love of God; because you can't.

I can honestly say that despite Steve's background, he was extremely attentive, loving and kind to me and my son during this time and frequently turned up at all hours to spend time with us. Perhaps it's difficult to understand the criminal mind for some, but Steve proves that a huge majority of men, no matter what their circumstances, can have a softer internal side.

He was involved with some very dangerous people and as I look back on some instances I can see God's hand upon everything. It was only by His grace and His will that I survived! At that time I hadn't seen anything that could be perceived as perilous but I was, as they say, blinded by love. There were many 'action-packed' evenings with Steve but one particular date night turned out to be the most extreme of eye-openers and the only one I will acknowledge. Steve and I were invited to an out of town event and it was to be a glamorous dress code. I remember during the day buying a beautiful silver-grey long satin dress and I felt fabulous as I prepared my hair and make-up for the evening. We arrived and met up with friends and champagne was flowing, along with laughter and chat. Half way through the event, a gang of rough looking men entered the gathering and quite literally started attacking people, throwing tables over and running around as though they were looking for someone. It was absolutely frightful and events occurred so quickly that before I knew it I found myself lying in a fetal position on the floor as three men kicked and punched me all over my body and head. Blow after blow pounding down upon me. I could feel distinct pain in my head and I thought I was going to die. It felt as though it lasted for hours yet it was, in reality, seconds. Then it stopped. I lay still and in my mind I thought I had to pretend I was dead or unconscious at the least, but at the same time was wondering if I was about to die. I could feel liquid trickling down all over my face. It was blood, from my head, my nose and my mouth. I thought this is it. I AM dead. What had just happened? I could hear screeching, shouting, glass breaking; and as the melee evolved around me, the survival instinct arose inside; adrenalin pumped and I knew I had to go. Now! I had to run, whatever happened! Within seconds, I turned my escape from a discreet crawl into a run. I didn't know where to run but I was in the pitch black open air before I knew it.

It was horrific, and as I turned around in the darkness I could see people being attacked and screaming and shouting. I was disorientated as I was not in my own town and didn't know where to go. I couldn't go back inside and I was concerned about where Steve was. In shock, bleeding and shaking from head to toe, I staggered a couple of blocks away from the venue. Then, I took off my heels and I ran. I was crying silently; wondering was this real; where do I go; is somebody following me? I didn't even turn to look. I just ran and before I needed to run any further I saw lights and I was on a main street. By the grace of God, I saw a taxi office and I was just thankful they could get me home instantly. I must have looked absolutely terrible and the driver asked me for the fare before we even started travelling. I had to explain what happened and when I say God was with me, I really mean it, as the driver still looked uncertain and I promised him I had money at my house.

I entered my home and struggled to the bathroom. I was aching, bruised and sore and I probably had a concussion. I ran a hot bath and sank into water, my skin stinging with the pain but I was home; I was alive. I don't even remember going to sleep that night but I woke up with a battered purple head, face and body the next day and a fear so embedded inside me, that I felt like a little girl all over again. No longer did the beautiful, silver-grey satin dress adorn my body. Now, it was a thick, enveloping fear that adorned me and I was unable to undress from this garment. This garment clung to my skin for many, many years.

****

At around 2pm the next day my phone rang. I cautiously answered and it was the girlfriend of one of Steve's friends. She called to tell me that she had found my gold locket on the floor from the previous night. She knew it meant the world to me as it had a photo of Samuel in it and I never took it off. After a very brief chat at the horror of the previous evening we agreed to meet up at a café in the town. To be honest, I was exceptionally apprehensive following the night before and didn't want to venture out of my home at all but I desperately wanted to get my locket back, so I made arrangements for a friend to come and watch over Samuel and I exited my home.

Jill was already waiting for me at the café with a hot cup of tea. I could see the shock on her face when she saw my injuries. She proceeded to tell me that the entire incident had been a matter of 'mistaken identity'. I didn't feel in my heart that it was true. I knew that I personally was a mistaken identity but I did feel that the group of men we shared company with were a definite and probable cause. But then she began to to tell me something I could never have expected to hear.

"Ellie, I need to tell you something. I think you should know. The minute those men entered the

room and started attacking everyone, Steve walked out of a side door. He knew there was going to be big trouble and he left you there. Ellie, he knew what those men were capable of and he abandoned you, he just left you"

On top of the horror of the previous twenty four hours, to have that information fired into my soul like a bullet was as sickening as every physical blow I had endured. I was devastated and nausea consumed me from within.

I didn't hear from Steve for days and I made no effort whatsoever to contact him. I could have been hospitalised or even dead! Although, sincerely, I knew that he would know exactly where I was. He had his sources. I was utterly heartbroken and it proved to me that the love I thought I had found wasn't real after all. This only compounded the distorted viewpoint I possessed already of love and I knew what I had to do. When he did eventually contact me I told him that I didn't want him in my life anymore.

I was about to learn that it was not going to be so simple to remove Steve from my life. He was not an easy person to say no to and he took it very badly. He threatened to burn down my house with me and Samuel in it; he would leave cryptic messages on my car; he would turn up very late in the evening, banging and shouting at my door. I was being intimidated again and again. I even moved house because I was petrified that he would fulfill his threats, but deep within, my resolve to do the right thing; my integrity intact; I persisted to turn him down each time until eventually he did give up and did not come around anymore…….

****

It wasn't since school days that I could remember ever discussing in detail any religious philosophies and with all his criminal associations and activities, it would seem Steve would be the last person I would have deep discussions with about God. Steve had spent ten years in prison at one point of his life and he told me he had read the Bible the whole way through on a few occasions. Whilst Steve kept bad company and he was indeed 'bad company' himself, he had a genuine humane side. I know after reading the preceding chapter you could find this a hard concept to digest, but I always have and probably always will, discover a snippet of goodness in everyone. I have memories of Steve which I choose to replace any horrific ones. I recall how we would stay up for hours when Samuel had gone to bed, discussing philosophy, travel, adventure and life itself. I have often thought upon this and perhaps I was the only one he could talk to about his unfulfilled dreams and ambitions. I now believe he probably wrestled constantly with his demons. But Steve was addicted to violence and not earning a living, but stealing it.

Years later I was driving my blue soft top Jeep one day through the town that I had once lived in; the town where I had spent those three years in the warped company of Steve. It was incredible but I saw him! Walking down a main road. I don't know why I did it, but I beeped my car horn and stopped. He got into the car and suddenly I couldn't feel anything but pity. He had dramatically changed, his entire demeanour had altered. He proceeded to tell me that he had an unhealthy heart and that he had very recently undergone heart bypass surgery and he had almost died. I drove him home and we chatted as old friends. I began to happily witness to him as to how I was now saved and how Jesus loved me and I loved Him and that I had found a new life. I was excited and wanted him to know that he could feel like this and become a new creation; a new person in Christ!

I thought he was about to agree as he opened his mouth to speak. But he said something I wasn't expecting at all. He said;

"Ellie, you know you were always the sunshine in my life. Whenever I was with you, it was like the sun was shining"

I turned to him and smiled. We reached our destination. I said a prayer for Steve. I would never see him again.

'"Do not seek revenge or bear a grudge against anyone among your people, but love your neighbor as yourself. I am the LORD.' Leviticus 19:18

Chapter 7: Radio Days

'Listen to counsel and accept discipline, That you may be wise the rest of your days. Many plans are in a man's heart, But the counsel of the LORD will stand.' Proverbs 19: 20-21

I continued to see my mother on occasion over the years that followed. We didn't have the best of relationships. We could have been closer perhaps and there were definitely times when we managed to cultivate a decent mother-daughter relationship but I almost feel that my mother didn't even like me and I suppose the fact that we lived such separate lives generated our inability to connect. Whenever I've pondered over our failure to maintain a loving relationship, I've come to the conclusion that when you have two damaged people, whether blood family or not, you feel you're in a continual atmosphere of deterioration. She had so much mental, emotional pain and sorrow inside of her that I couldn't see and I had so much confusion, depredation, and shame inside of me that she only knew the half of. God's Word teaches us about being unequally yoked in marriage and the possible consequences. Being unequally yoked with anyone is a choice but not one of us chose our parents or the families we are born into. Although as I write that sentence I am so aware of the fact, now, that God did choose the family in which we would be placed and every birth upon this earth is only at his acquiescence. It's because of the voluminous barrier in our relationship I believe, that when my mother gave me some devastating news one day, I reacted with an appalling indifference.

"Ellie, I need you to know something. I've been diagnosed with breast cancer. I have to have surgery and radiotherapy so I'm going to be absent from work for quite a while too."

I didn't even flinch. By now I was in my mid-twenties and I thought, erroneously, that if I didn't absorb that information then I didn't have to deal with it! My way of reaching out to her was suggesting that with the extra time she had now she could help me with Samuel! I look back on that moment with utter shame. How could I have suggested something like that when she had a life-threatening condition? Although unwarranted however, I should disclose that I had developed over time a kind of defence system that enabled me to go into automatic pilot. I could almost live like a 'Stepford wife' – robotic and unfeeling. However, unlike the real Stepford wife I possessed the ability to fool people and they wouldn't notice any difference.

I had managed to remain the life and soul of the party. Everyone still called me 'Smiler' and my friends would always seek me out for help and advice in any life issues or problems they needed solving. I think it was because, as I still am today, an avid reader, with a library full of self-help books! I debated regularly with friends on psychological issues and possible solutions to any of their concerns. I absorbed every word of any new age type books and would read and explore any knowledge I could, especially if I thought it could rid me of fear, shame, depressive thoughts and suicidal ideation. Now, it's a blessing to have bookshelves of Bibles and studies of theology and Christian doctrine. What a difference!

I would not only live every minute to the full but would try to control everyone around me into the bargain. I had mutated into a person who cared but didn't want to show it fully. I was afraid others would see my faults and I didn't like that thought. I had a serious underlying depression and I guess it was my way of not only trying to cope, but also overcome. I would again, continually turn to my Tarot cards for guidance thus I had no peace at all and a false sense of identity that projected itself as a confident Ellie who didn't let anything faze her. My way of coping with this was to work; work very hard, and I did!
I was not saved and therefore Jesus was not the cornerstone or centre of my life. My son Samuel was

the centre of my life and my mission and deepest desire was being a good mummy to Samuel; being a long distance runner whenever I had a second of spare time and working hard at my job. I have always been what we call in the UK, a 'grafter' i.e. a hard worker. I needed to be that too! Not just for financial reasons because I was studying law but because I also liked to compose music and record and that required extra money. Even though I had an idea what I wanted to fulfill career wise, music and song gave me an escape. Because I was immersing myself working full time, studying, running, recording music and being a mother, there was not much time to dwell on any deep-seated emotional issues that existed.

After my mother's recent disclosure, being so engrossed in a busy life also helped me to detach myself from the knowledge that I belonged to a long line of generational cancer sufferers in my family. With my mother's diagnosis now unveiled, I was very aware that I was in line to be the 4th generation of my maternal family line to have cancer in their 30's or 40's. My great grandfather had died at the age of 36 years old from liver cancer; his daughter (my maternal grandmother) had suffered womb cancer at 37 years old; her sister had leukemia in her late forties and now my mother had breast cancer in her forties too. I now had to confront the fact that I may get cancer at an early age also and this terrified me. Isn't it strange that I spent so many years thinking that I wanted to exit the earth, yet the fear of a life threatening illness caused me nothing but terror and angst.

One precious and life-changing joy for me when I first accepted Jesus as my Lord and Saviour was knowing that in the Bible it says that "The cure for a 'generational curse' is repentance of the sin in question, faith in Christ, and a life consecrated to the Lord" (Romans 12:1-2). I do not live in fear of any sickness or cancer now and know that sickness is of the enemy and not of God.

****

I used to love spending time at the recording studio. I had a brilliant technician, Paul, and he would recommend me for backing vocals with various bands that came into the studio. He also had his own band and he would ask me to come along and watch them at concerts and gigs, then in the middle of the event he would say to a large audience;

"I have my friend Ellie here tonight and she is going to sing!"

Then he would take me onto the stage and have me sing; Acapella normally! Always tricking me onto the stage but in a charming and presumable way! He knew I loved to get lost in a world of my own, only ever singing the songs that were implanted deeply into my heart. We used to work on a lot of stuff together and I can honestly say they were some of the most memorable, sweet and fulfilling times of my twenties; of my unsaved life. I still have a few recordings that my daughter can't get enough of and that makes me smile! The recording studio was eight miles away from my home so I used my time getting there as a great opportunity for a good run. Then I would take a breather and relax for a while at the studio. We were like a little family and spent so much time laughing. We would proceed with whatever was planned for the next few hours and I would either get a lift home or run again.

It's funny how you can remember specific days so clearly in your life, that you recall how you felt; what you were wearing; even the weather, isn't it? On one of these particular days, around September time, I had run over to the studio as usual. I had on a sky blue running top and my favourite battered running trainers, my Ron Hill leggings and my hair was thrown up in a ponytail. I was feeling powerful and free and looking forward to getting something on tape. YES! It was on tape! We did use CD's but were also still using tapes at that time and I have always kept my tapes and an old well used tape recorder! The song I recall we were working on was called *'We forgot to feed ourselves.'* It was about taking everything into our bodies except love; to me, the real food. I think I called it vitamin 'L'. Wow! I should re-read my abundance of song lyrics from that time; I wonder what they will possibly reveal??

As I walked into the studio, I noticed Paul sitting with two young men, both very good-looking and they seemed to be relishing some comical interaction together. Paul was a hilarious character and so I walked in and felt comfortable enough to start chatting along with them. Paul said he had just been telling Curtis, one of the guys, about me. I noticed that Curtis just kept staring at me. He was there to record a song but he was actually a drummer and had a passionate and talented way! We started to talk about songs we loved and what Curtis was planning to record and we all hit it off really well. His friend Martin had come along to support Curtis and I thought he was adorable. In fact, I was very attracted to him. Although Martin wasn't to be the one

I became close to. It seems almost inconceivable to me now, but I was not attracted to Curtis at all!

The meeting itself though was a lovely, innocent introduction and would turn out to be the beginning of my knowledge of God and a series of life changing events!

****

Over time I noticed that it was becoming a regular occurrence, that whenever I turned up at the studio, Curtis would be there. It was only weeks later that I discovered through Paul's divulgence, that when Curtis discovered I was a regular at the studio, he asked Paul to coincide all his recordings with mine, so that he would accidentally bump into me as I arrived. This makes me giggle now as I write! I started to look forward to seeing him, never guessing that it was all a plan and here is where you can distinctly see the difference between good manipulation and bad. Curtis was manipulating events to see me but his intentions were wholesome and good, whereas in the past people manipulated events to create a very different effect. As I've said before, something can be right in front of me and I don't see it and Curtis was right in front of me doing everything he could to spend time with me and become a part of my life and I didn't even have a clue! When you don't value yourself so much and have a low self-esteem, even if you have a slight idea that someone would go out of their way to see you, it would only ever be a fleeting thought and nothing you could ever believe as solid. Because why would someone want to go out of their way to see me? And that's how I speculated regarding any attention. Therefore, my mind had convinced me that no-one would be inclined to desire me as I believed that everybody else knew I was as worthless as I felt.

But one day, the feelings Curtis had were confirmed! He and I were sitting and talking as we always did at the studio and he just looked at me and blurted out,

"I'm going to marry you one day!'"

I was shocked but flattered all at the same time! It definitely hit an emotional spot and very swiftly we began what would become a passionate, intimate but inexorably co-dependent relationship. I explain with depth the co-dependence as I discovered Curtis had not had the easiest of childhoods either. He had a good hardworking mother but a father who had repeatedly walked in and out of his life, gradually affecting Curtis' behaviour and self-worth. I cannot tell Curtis' story. That's not my place or business but I will say this; that after many years of loving each other hard and then hating each other hard, back and forth, back and forth, we are now parents to a wonderful and stable daughter, who we parent very well together even though we are not a couple. I would go so far as to say, we are also good friends and I know Curtis agrees. When two individuals join together, who are in effect, inexperienced and also without either ever having had cultivated examples when it comes to handling a mature love relationship, it can only cause grief and pain, whether initially or eventually. A good relationship isn't based on passion, lust and desperation. It's based on friendship, respect and most of all, Jesus. But we were young and we thought we were in love. Each of us provided something the other needed, at that time.

Nonetheless, this relationship was one of the most important in my life from the perspective that Curtis was the first person to ever discuss God with me in a 'born-again' way. He demonstrated this to me by his perception of God as his Father, his friend and someone you could know and trust. Curtis would talk about having a relationship with God. I didn't really fully understand him at the time but I listened purely because I love deep spiritual conversations and I like to learn and glean from people so I would ask him to tell me more and would be completely engrossed. Our conversations would leave me deep in thought and analysing for hours.

It was apparent that Curtis was a very good father figure to Samuel and over time we decided to live together. The closer we got, or should I say, the more dependent we became on each other; like me, Curtis would want to run away from the relationship. He couldn't handle a sophisticated, adult relationship at that time and it got to the stage where whenever he would leave, I knew he would be back knocking on the door three days later. It was always three days! And of course I would take him back. It was so very damaging to me though; it was back and forth, back and forth. It wasn't good for me and it wasn't good for Samuel. However, I allowed it and I wish I'd had the strength to stop it then, but whenever you're not living a Godly and wise life, you allow situations to keep returning and we tend to become 'repeat offenders'.

I'm not saying any of this was Curtis' fault and I'm not saying it was mine either. In fact, we rarely argued; it was just one big emotional, confusing mess. I think the only big argument we ever had was over me chopping mushrooms the wrong way!! I know! We can laugh now, but at the time it was a horrible fight about the mushrooms! The underlining factor here though, is the pain is always under the surface and there's a reason why silly arguments like this can start. It's a pressure cooker scenario.

So, here we were, Samuel, Curtis and I and of course it was me who thought it would be a great idea to have another baby. I thought it would create a proper family…..oh dear! It's strange though because Curtis used to say to me;

"If we ever have a baby, it'll be a little girl".

Do you know, it wasn't until I was saved, that I found out that Curtis had actually given his life to Jesus years before, at the young age of eleven? He'd even received the gift of tongues. Then his life had taken a downward spiral when the enemy had most definitely come in to attack and he was completely backslidden for many years. Here is where I am enlightened with the fact that once you have 'known' God and felt the power of the Holy Spirit, no matter if you turn away from God, He has never taken His hand from you. That was why Curtis was always talking to me about this 'relationship' with God.

Something we did have in common was motorbikes and we were about to go on holiday to the Greek island of Zakynthos when I discovered I was five weeks pregnant. I was twenty-nine years old and five years older than Curtis. We did have an amazing holiday and were on the motorbike for the whole week driving around just one of the stunning, idyllic Greek islands. Then on the last day of the holiday I was very sick. I was convinced it couldn't possibly be morning sickness but unfortunately it was a form of pregnancy sickness and when we got back to the UK I had to be taken into hospital. I spent the next seven months in hospital apart from the few odd days I was allowed home. I had an abhorrent sickness called Hyperemesis Gravadarum. I was so very poorly; it spoiled the joy at my pregnancy. I was constantly away from Samuel and that made me heartsick but I knew that he and Curtis were a happy little team.

It came to the stage that if something could go wrong with my body, it did. Blood clots, dehydration, collapsing, you name it; it happened. Plus, I didn't even look like myself. I remember looking in a mirror at the hospital and I felt confused because it wasn't me looking back! I didn't recognise myself. I could write a full chapter on how awful that sickness was but I won't. When I first heard the news about Prince William's wife, Kate, suffering from the same sickness, I thought "Oh my word, she's going through hell and nobody understands the intensity of it". I prayed hard for her. Hyperemesis Gravadarum is a hugely misunderstood sickness and isn't just a bad case of morning sickness. There were times I was so poorly that my consultant disclosed I was the worst case he had ever known. Why am I not surprised? I really thought I was going to die at times. It isn't a life threatening condition unless a woman isn't treated quickly and fortunately in this era we have access to instant medical care if living in a wealthy country.

We found out our baby was due towards the end of March, 2001. We had decided to find out the sex and it was as Curtis had said; it would be a girl! Arriving just under 3 weeks early and weighing almost eight and a half pounds, with jet black hair and the most beautiful golden skin was Rhiannon Eve. Oh wow! She was awesome and so healthy looking. I could see that even though I'd been terribly sick and weak, this robust yet exquisite little angel had drawn out of me every bit of goodness that she could! But holding her in my arms made every moment of pain worth it! She was indescribably beautiful and adorable and she still is; even as a teenager!

However, immediately after Rhiannon was born my body encountered further trauma and I hemorrhaged losing a high volume of blood very quickly. I suffered from hypovolemic shock and my body was almost completely shutting down. I know Curtis did an awful lot of praying and was holding our brand new baby in his arms, wondering if her mother would be alright. God obviously and thankfully answered his prayers. It was yet another harrowing and death-defying encounter in my own life and an alarming situation for Curtis. Even though I was saved from death, the part that makes me so sad is my inability to breastfeed Rhiannon. I've always been upset about that as it was one of the multitude of close and precious times with Samuel when he was a baby. However, Rhiannon was healthy and a very contented new born and we were extremely thankful for that. It took me a great deal of time to recover from everything my body had contended with for the previous nine months but it was within the following months, that unknown to me, I was about to experience the most dramatic and life changing encounter of my whole life.

****

'Ellie, you're horrible, ugly, a no good mother, kill yourself, it's the best way, you can't do this, you're incapable, rubbish, a no good worthless mess.'

These were the thoughts I grappled with day after day. Not voices from the outside, just continual thoughts and whisperings of my own. Within days, I had sunk into a deep, deep, postnatal depression. It was horrific. I wanted to die, but my powerful love connection was ALWAYS there with my children. I wouldn't EVER have left them, but the feelings were there to end it all and they were real, very real. The suicidal ideation had begun again. It was pure and utter torment. Curtis was perturbed and tormented that he couldn't make thing better for me and he was doing everything he could to make life as normal as possible for Samuel and Rhiannon. I'll never forget one day I accused him of wanting to kill the children. That man went through hell but yet he kept trying to help me. There were so many incidents but I can't possibly go into them; they are too numerous to mention. Even so the remarkable thing was that though I was seriously ill, and obviously my physical body was still recovering, I managed to still put my children and their needs ahead of my own and that is what saved my life. My children WERE MY LIFE. I loved so hard but I could feel myself unravelling more and more. Even as I write these very words I'm filling with tears as I recall that awful time.

Depression is truly devastating and beyond doubt a horrific illness to endure. I'm not talking about anxiety issues here; although they can be as debilitating. I'm not talking feeling the blues; or feeling glum. This was, again, another depression and a very real and very dangerous illness. You can only put on the façade for a reasonable amount of time before it takes over everything.

But then came the day...

Chapter 8: Salvation's Song

'For it is with your heart that you believe and are justified,
and it is with your mouth that you profess your faith and are
saved.' Romans 10:10

As I encountered those darkest of days, it was the most paradoxical of times and I can't begin to explain the utter joy at being a new mother again and how blessed I felt at having a little boy and a little girl.   Although beset with physical and mental depression it was the support of Curtis and certain friends that really helped me through and when I say I loved my little children; I mean the intensity of my love was smothering. The tormented concerns I had been overwhelmed with when Samuel was a baby returned intensely and one day I broke down in front of Curtis and told him how frightened I was of all the evil in the world and that something terrible might happen to Rhiannon. I do know that many mothers experience these fears and Curtis tried everything he could, literally cosseting me in love and always encouraging me as a mother. He would tell me I was the best mother ever and he wouldn't have wanted anyone else to be his child's mother. He constantly spoke about my skills as a mother to Samuel and Rhiannon; to everyone he met. But deep down, and as I look back now, he was more than likely at his wits end and trying to do the right thing. I realised years later that our already damaged relationship was being held together by the thread of responsibility for the children and a heap of pity. I believe Curtis had fallen out of love with me long before but was anxious that possibly one more issue could tip me over the edge.

I have to point out we had the most amazing times in the first year of Rhiannon's life and I don't want to make it all seem doom and gloom. At the heart of it, we were best friends and loved being parents and maintaining a family life together.

But sadly, at the same time, I was caught up with events and fears from my past; with the reality that I couldn't always protect my children; with tensions, pressures and a fear so heavy it was as though I was carrying a load of bricks around with me all day, every day; just the way I felt as a child at one time. Fear isn't just emotional; it's a physical burden too.

Soon, very soon, the enemy knew that the time was coming when I would be welcomed into the Kingdom of God, where I would have access to a life of joy, peace and righteousness and I can see how he was desperate to hang on to this wretched soul of mine. His stronghold upon me was vigorous and his way of keeping my mind living in the past was powerful.

I was at my wits end…………..

✳✳✳✳✳✳✳✳✳

"She sat in her little green car, deathly still, an overflow of tears still racing down her cheeks, her chest, her body shuddering,

not constantly now but with the occasional shake a lament brings, not a howl or a wail anymore. Her body had succumbed to the deep rooted pain that was submerged far far beneath the exterior of this woman. She felt spent. Completely debilitated. She could barely speak the words she wanted to say..... But she sensed these words had to be declared! Had to be roared! She would shout out these words as soon as she could. But right at that moment, she couldn't even form her lips to speak.

There was torrential rain all around and she had driven into a huge park grounds, trees were everywhere. Whenever she was walking amongst trees, she felt a calm; nature reminded her of her Grandfather..........And rain; she loved rain. Still does. A joy arises in her to this day when there is a downpour or thunderstorm.

But not that day. That day had turned out to be the catalyst. It was THE day. The turning point.

That day, grief, fear and despair had all accumulated and the pain of the last 29 years had become a mass; a concentrated mass of anguish, misery and wretchedness. She had to get rid of it! How do I get it out? She thought. What do I do? The pain was physical. It caused her to not breathe at times. A lifetime of hurts and atrocities had hit her all at once……..and something had to give.

And so…………she screamed out……..to a God she didn't know. To a God who she wasn't even sure existed. To a God Who was waiting……..for His little girl…..for THIS moment. "HELP. I CAN'T LIVE ANYMORE. I CAN'T DO THIS LIVING THING. I CAN'T LEAVE MY BABIES. SO WHAT DO I DO? IF YOU ARE REAL, IF YOU ARE LOOKING NOW, HELP ME, HELP ME PLEASE. DO SOMETHING PLEASE. PLEASE JUST HELP ME."

And He did……………..

****

It was 3 days after I had taken my drive to the countryside to calm my nerves and reach out………to someone.

Quite out of the blue Curtis suggested I visit a local salon; to pamper myself; have my hair and nails done and generally treat myself. Even though I've always had an obsession almost, with hygiene and being groomed well, for the previous few months I hadn't treated myself in any way and Curtis thought it would revive me and cheer me up.

I really didn't feel like it and it also meant I would be away from the children for a few hours, which didn't appeal to me but eventually I agreed and walked about a mile away to enquire for appointments at a salon.

It was just like any regular shop on the outside and as I looked through the window is seemed quite empty. Because of this I felt safe enough to go inside. I began to warm up to the idea of spending time on myself and relaxing.

As I entered through the door I saw a tall and glamorous blonde lady looking up at me from the reception. Would you understand me if I said it looked as though she had a glow all around her and that she was almost floating? It felt like I had walked into a soft, hazy atmosphere and that radiance was filling the whole room.

The only way I can explain it, is I felt 'shielded'. I was walking into a supernatural atmosphere but I wasn't aware of that at the time.

The lady said, *"Hello, my love"* and smiled a gentle smile. As I look back now, I realise it was a perceptive and knowing smile.

I said, *"Hi".*

She furthered,

"I knew you were coming; God told me........Oh my word, my love; you've got four angels,' (and with that she used her finger to point in strategic positions around me), *'all around you......Oh my love; oh bless you love; I'm glad you're here."*

Bewildered, astounded, stunned and shocked! Well, those aren't even the words! I had never seen this woman before in my life yet my mind immediately recalled those moments in the car park where I had cried out to God, in the depths of my despair, only three days before. Called out to a God I could not see, but whom others had told me loved me unconditionally; and He had answered me! He had answered Ellie! He was waiting for me at the salon. He was waiting for His little girl. And oh boy, did I run into His arms!

You might think that it could've just been a very strange and coincidental encounter but the second I had walked into the salon I was, I now know, enveloped in a supernatural atmosphere; like the air was different. And this woman was a vessel, used by the Lord. And most importantly, she had obeyed His leading.

The lady's name, I'm proud to share with you, is Andrina. She is still, to this day, a confidante, a mentor, and a close friend. Her side of the story is also incredible. Andrina is very musical and very prophetic. What had happened just prior to me arriving at her shop that day was that God had given her a specific word and told her to expect me. This in itself blew me away and I just had to know more! My life was changing in that salon and I needed to know how God could arrange this!

As our conversation progressed Andrina invited me to go to a church. It would be my first visit. I could not wait to tell Curtis what had happened and I returned that day from the salon a very different Ellie than the one that walked in – no more despair, no more depression, and no more hopelessness. All these things had been replaced with hope, joy and thankfulness.

On my first visit to the church, I gave my life, heart and soul to Jesus. I didn't hesitate! The decision was easy and I was hungry for salvation. I was hungry and desperate to experience peace and love that surpasses all understanding. I was hungry to have what God offered and not what the world offered, for the first time in my life! I was hungry, full stop!

On the first visit to the church, I had taken Samuel with me and he also got saved the same night; he was nine years old! My little first born, precious boy was also accepting of the gift of salvation through Jesus. Our lives were changing. It was a new path we had taken and we were bathed in pure love.

That night I felt the presence of angels all around me and that never left. At last I was safe. At last I could be Ellie, the new creation in Christ – as I uttered the sinner's prayer, the pain of the past seemed to melt away with every word.

"I TRY TO BE LIKE A FOREST: REVITALISING AND CONSTANTLY GROWING"

Forest Whitaker

Epilogue

Its 14 years since I was saved. I have gone from being an abused and emotional walking time bomb to a woman who is constantly rooted in Christ. However, it hasn't been an easy journey.

My story of those 14 years will be the subject matter of my next book 'I Smile'. I've had the Lord with me all through these last 14 years but I had to endure one of the most devastating and traumatic incidences of my whole life.

I will share with you the ups and downs, how the enemy came in to steal, kill and destroy, again. And what happened next.......Thank you and God bless you.

Ellie Palma-Cass

Salvation Prayer

'If the words in this book have spoken to you and you want to invite Jesus into your heart please pray the following prayer'

"Dear Father in Heaven. I believe you sent Jesus, your one and only Son, to die on the Cross for my sins and for my ultimate salvation. I am so thankful that Jesus shed His precious blood so that I may live eternally with You in Heaven. Father God, I turn away from all my past sins and ask for your forgiveness. Please come into my heart right now, as I confess Jesus as my Lord and Saviour from this day forward"

If you have prayed this prayer and committed your life to Jesus, the next step is to find a local Christian church for fellowship and growing your faith.

'I am praying with you and for you! Love Ellie'

About the Author

Ellie Palma-Cass is a devoted mother, trusted friend to many, ministry leader, author, and speaker. She has worked as the UK representative for an international ministry/organisation and been a committed personal assistant to a world renowned American preacher.

Ellie is the founder of elliepalmacass.com ministries and is intrinsically involved with her team and the aims and development of the ministry as she seeks to serve her God-given purpose in an international way. *"Therefore go and make disciples of all nations, baptising them in the name of the Father and of the Son and of the Holy Spirit"* (Matt 28:19. NIV)

The ethos of the ministry is purely 'to be used as God's vessel to save souls.'

As well as her dynamic and dedicated approach to speaking and writing, Ellie has a calling to 'love the unlovely' and prefers a 'hands on' approach wherein she partakes in regular mission trips around the world; her hope to reach many and praying that God will use her to touch even the *one*.

Ellie lives in the North of England and loves spending time with her daughter, long distance running, eating cheesecake (this is where the running helps!), playing the harmonica, has an extensive and eclectic love of music including Reggae and French jazz, travelling, reading, interior design and Harley Davidsons! She basically loves life and it's all with thanks to our Lord and Saviour Jesus Christ!

CONTACT ELLIE

www.elliepalmacass.com

For Speaking Engagements | Book Signings
Email: info@elliepalmacass.com

For United States enquiries please email DBC
Agency Writers:

Email: dbcagency@outlook.com

19271188R00107

Printed in Great Britain
by Amazon